KEEPSAKES

Dedication

I dedicate this book to all those
countless home cooks whom continuously
put a meal on the table with flair, grace
grace, & often with an inventiveness
that is called for when trying to figure
out what to make for dinner.

Regal
731M - 18

.. forget me not

Frances Hansen

KEEPSAKES

RECIPES MEMENTOS MISCELLANY

FRANCES HANSEN

CONTENTS:

BAKING

Hokey pokey biscuits
Afghans
Tamarillo & cinnamon pie
Feijoa loaf
Rocky road
Butterscotch slice
Queen cakes
Currant cakes
Pikelets
Butterfly cakes
Lemon meringue pie
Dorset apple cake
Large chocolate cake
Carrot & apple cake
Ginger slice
Tracey's boiled fruit loaf
Raisin loaf
Apple shortcake

PUDDINGS

Pavlova
Lemon delicious
Bread & butter pudding
Banana splits with hot
 chocolate sauce
Feijoa & banana crumble
Chocolate fudge pudding
Baked custard
Aunty Hazel's cheesecake
Rice pudding
Sponge for hot fruit

WEIGHTS & MEASUREMENTS

Butter

1 cup	250g
1 tablespoon (Tblesp or T)	15g
1 dessertspoon (D)	10g

Flour

2 cups (C)	300g
2 tablespoons	15g
2 dessertspoons	10g

Sugar

1 cup	250g
1 tablespoon	15g
1 dessertspoon	10g

Other

1000 grams	1 kilogram
100 grams	3.5 ounces
1000 millilitres	1 litre

OVEN SETTINGS

	°Fahrenheit	°Celsius
Very Cool	225 - 275	110 - 140
Cool	300 - 325	150 - 160
Moderate	350 - 375	180 - 190
Hot	400 - 450	200 - 230
Very Hot	475 - 500	250 - 260

OUNCES	GRAMS
1	30
2	60
3	90
4	125
5	155
10	315
16 (1 lb)	455

FLUIDS

1 cup	=250 ml
1 tsp	=5 ml
1 T	=20 ml

soups

Parengarenga Harbour

Rangaunu Bay

Ninety-mile Beach

Cavalli Is.

Awanui

Bay of Islands

Cape Brett

Kaikohe

Kawakawa

Hokianga Harbour

Poor Knights Is.

Whangarei Harbour

Mokohinau Is.

Ruakaka

Hen and Chicken Is.

Mangawhai

Great Barrier

Little Barrier I.

Cuvier

Kaipara Harbour

Merc

Muriwai Beach

AUCKLAND

Coromandel Pen.

Oaia I.

Manukau Harbour

Firth of Thames

Awhitu Pen.

Karaka

Hauraki Plains

L. Waikare

Raglan Harbour

Tauranga

Gannet I.

WITHDRAWN

Presented to the

Papakura Public Library

by

Auckland Savings Bank

on the occasion of the

OFFICIAL OPENING on the

8th day of August, 1969

Ham & Pea Soup   (Mum)

ham or bacon bones
1 cup soup mix
½ cup barley
1 onion, diced finely

Cover ham/bacon bones with water
in a large pot. Add the soup mix,
barley and onion.
Simmer for 1&1/2 hours
Remove meat from the bones and return
tto soup.

3 sticks celery, finely sliced
2 large carrots, grated
2 small parsnips, grated
2 medium sized potatoes, cut into
small cubes

Add the above vegetables totthe soup.
Season with plenty of S&P, a dash of
soya sauce, or a cube of vegetable
stock for extra flavour.

Mushroom + Hazelnut soup.

1. 50 g. butter
2. lg. onions, peeled chopped roughly
3. 3 cloves garlic crushed
4. 500 g mushrooms
5. 6 c chicken stock
6. lg potato peeled
7. 70 grams pk hazelnuts roasted + skinned.
8. 1 cup cream.

1. heat butter, add onions, garlic mushrooms + cook over mod heat till onions softened.
2. add chick stock + diced potato allow mix to stand
3. chop nuts
4. process soup & add nuts, add cream - simmer 5 mins' till thickened (poss. thicken with flour + butter

Corn Chowder:

3 rashers bacon
1 medium onion
2 cups chicken stock
1 sweet potato, peeled and diced
s&p
310g creamed corn
300g corn kernels, drained
1cup milk
½ tsp paprika,
½ cup sour cream
1 egg lightly beaten
Saute onion & bacon, add sweet potato, stock, s & p.
Simmer until sweet potato is nearly soft, add rest of ingredients,
adding the egg at the very end.
Serve immediately, piping hot with lots of fresh chopped flat leafed
parsley, lemon juice and more pepper & salt.

Corn Soup

8 cobs fresh corn
3 spring onions finely sliced
1 clove garlic finely sliced
1 cup cream
2 T olive oil
1 litre chicken stock

Method:
Cut corn off the cobs, this is easier if you
stand the cob upright and cut downwards
turning the cob as you go.
Saute garlic & corn in oil, adding stock
after a couple of minutes.
Blend with wand stick, slowly add in cream
stirring gently, do not boil, sprinkle with
the spring onions, squeeze of lemon juice to
finish.
Season with lots of Salt & pepper as you go.

Extra toppings:
Toasted pine nuts, chopped parsley,
coriander or basil, tiny bit of rosemary

Gourmet Corn Soup   (Mum)

This recipe is a bit of a joke in our family as Mum calls it gourmet
but really it is just so basic , centred around a pkt of frozen corn kernals.
The joke is......that is actually is very delicious:

1 pkt frozen corn kernals
1 cup milk
1 cup cream
Cook the corn in a little water for a few mins, add the milk & cream.
Blend, season with salt & pepper, garnish with snipped chives

Cream of Spinach Soup (Mary)

- 3 T chopped onion
- 2 cloves garlic, finely chopped
- 4 T. Butter
- 1 T. flour
- ½ litre chicken stock, vege stock or water.
- ½ kg fresh spinach or pkt. frozen spinach.
- 125 ml cream
- grated nutmeg
- 250 ml milk
- ½ tsp sugar
- Salt & pepper
- snipped chives
- 1 tin oyster pieces (optional - use canned oysters)

Cook onion & garlic gently in the butter with the lid on. When mixture golden, stir in the flour, then stock or water. Add spinach, cover & simmer 5 mins. Blend with wand stick.

Preheat adding milk & cream, check seasoning S&P, stir in oysters, garnish with nutmeg or chives (not both).

* Optional - Blend oysters as well if you don't like the chunky texture.
* Fresh oysters - use all juice - heat 3 mins max.

thermos

EIGHT DAYS A WEEK

VERSE 1

OOH (C) I NEED YOUR (D) LOVE BABE, (F) GUESS YOU KNOW IT'S TRUE (C)

--- (C) HOPE YOU NEED MY (D) LOVE BABE, (F) JUST LIKE I NEED YOU (C)

(Am) HOLD ME ------ (F) LOVE ME ------ (Am) HOLD ME ------ (D) LOVE ME -----

(C) AIN'T GOT NOTHIN BUT LOVE (D) BABE --- (F) EIGHT DAYS A WEEK (C)

VERSE 2

LOVE (C) YOU EV'RY (D) DAY GIRL, (F) ALWAYS ON MY MIND (C)

--- (C) ONE THING I CAN (D) SAY GIRL, (F) LOVE YOU ALL THE TIME (C)

(Am) HOLD ME ------ (F) LOVE ME ------ (Am) HOLD ME ------ (D) LOVE ME ------

(C) AIN'T GOT NOTHIN BUT LOVE (D) GIRL --- (F) EIGHT DAYS A WEEK (C)

CHORUS

(G) EIGHT DAYS A WEEK I LOVE (Am) YOU

(D7) EIGHT DAYS A WEEK IS (F) NOT ENOUGH TO (G) SHOW I CARE ------

REPEAT VERSE 1

REPEAT CHORUS

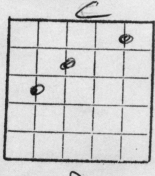

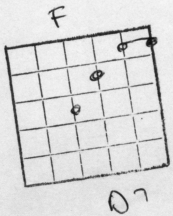

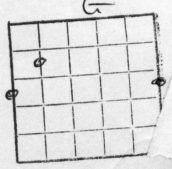

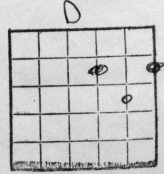

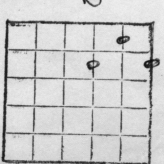

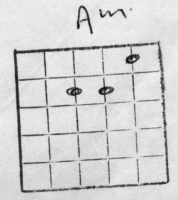

SUPER QUICK PEA SOUP

(Richard O.)

- OLIVE OIL
- GARLIC

- PEAS (FROZEN) ONE BAG

- WATER or STOCK TO COVER

- SALT & PEPPER

* COCONUT or OLIVE
OIL can be added
after.
FANCY

- SAUTEE OIL & GARLIC
- PLACE PEAS & WATER IN TILL THE BOIL
- PLACE IN BLENDER TILL SMOOTH
- ADD MORE LIQUID IF NEEDED

NEW ZEALAND SOUVENIRS

United Crafts

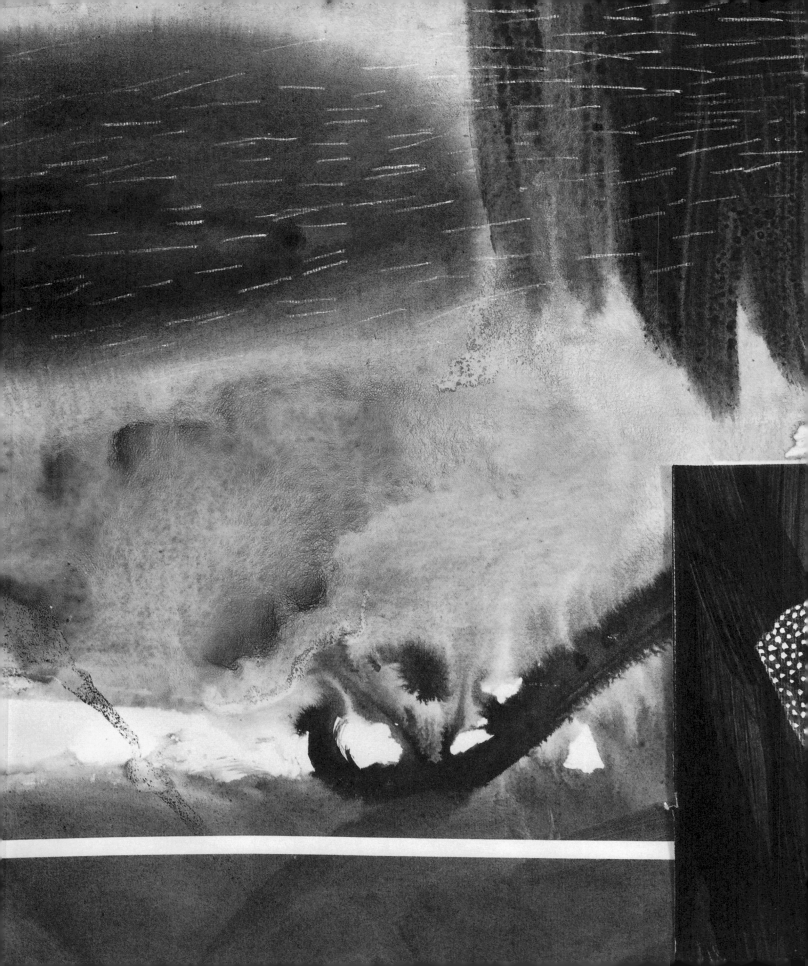

Black eyed Bean & Mushroom Soup

Ingredients:
2T butter
1 stick celery finely sliced
2 cloves garlic finely sliced
1 onion diced
400 gms mixed mushrooms
1 cup dried black eyed beans
1 cup lite cream
4 cups vege stock
1 T finely chopped italian parsley
salt & pepper
lemonjuice for serving

Saute celery, garlic & onion in butter on low heat, 5 mins.
Add mushrooms and a little of the stock, ½ cup, turn up the
heat. Add plenty of S&P.
When mushrooms are mostly cooked, (5 mins) add rest of stock
and the beans, which have been cooked separately, (30-40 min)
nb. beans will cook quicker if soaked overnite.
Blend soup with a wand stick, stopping when the mix is
still a little chunky, as this gives a nice texture.
Stir in cream, adjust seasoning.
Servewith a sprinkling of chopped parsley
and lemon juice.

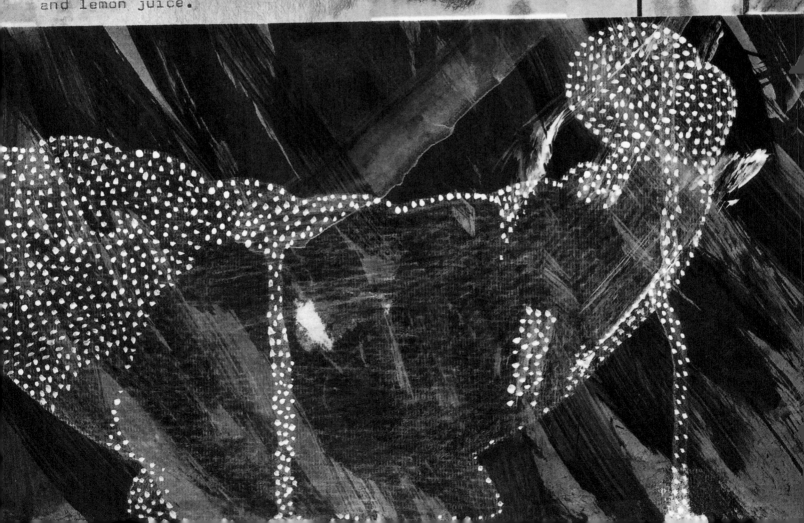

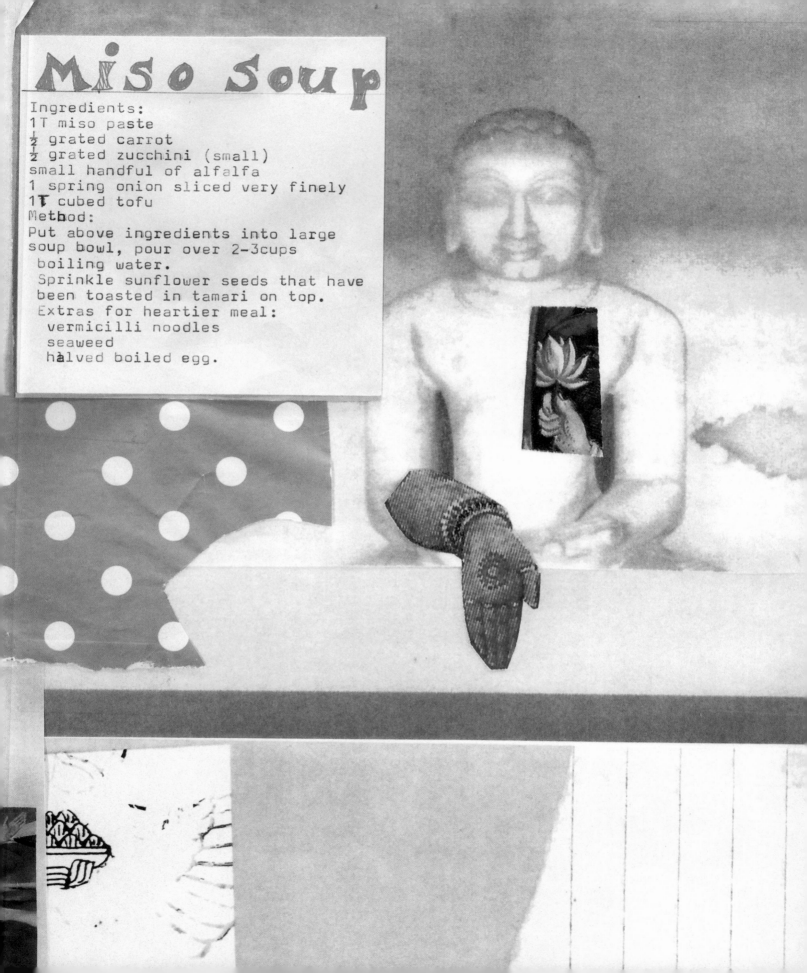

Miso Soup

Ingredients:
1T miso paste
½ grated carrot
½ grated zucchini (small)
small handful of alfalfa
1 spring onion sliced very finely
1T cubed tofu

Method:
Put above ingredients into large
soup bowl, pour over 2-3cups
boiling water.
Sprinkle sunflower seeds that have
been toasted in tamari on top.
Extras for heartier meal:
 vermicilli noodles
 seaweed
 halved boiled egg.

Note:
Miso Paste comes in
different colours
in 1g packets &
in individual serves.
Find it in the asian
section of your
supermarket.
This soup is an
excellent lunch on
a cold day, the cafe
at my artschool used
to make a version of
this. mmmmmmmmmmmmmm

Chicken & Vegetable Soup

Using an organic chicken, rinse thoroughly, put into a large
pot of water with a lemon that has been stabbed with a knife a
few times, (to let the juices run out), 2 large onions diced,
2-3 bay leaves and 2 cups of mixed grains such as barley,
yellow lentils and split peas.
You could also use the prepackaged soup mixes, country chicken
is a very apt one!
Season with plenty of freshly ground black pepper and sea
salt.
Simmer away, with lid on for 1-1½ hrs.

Meanwhile prepare all the vegetables:
2 large carrots grated,
1 parsnip, grated
3 zucchinis, grated
3 sticks celery, finely sliced
1 handful of fresh celery leaves finely chopped.

Skim off fatty froth from the surface, remove lemon and bay
leaves from the pot. Discard.
Remove chicken from the pot, this is tricky as it will be
falling apart. Carefully scoop up all the meat and bones from
the stock, cool and then strip away all the meat. You will
need to dice up the larger pieces.
Add all the veg to the pot, simmer for 30 mins, at this stage
you could add a large potato, peeled and diced, for a thicker,
heartier soup.
Add the cooked chicken meat.
Season with more S&P, juice of 1 lemon,
Serve with finely chopped Italian parsley, and bread for
dipping.

nb: You may need to
add more water
if the soup
gets too
thick.

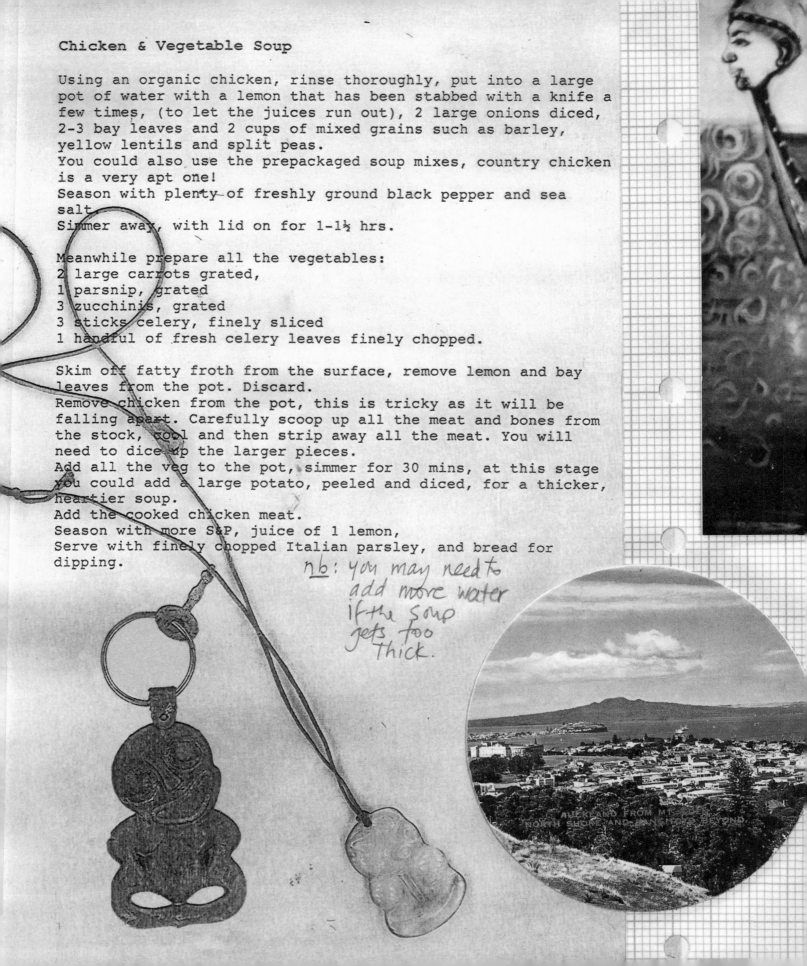

AUCKLAND FROM MT
NORTH SHORE AND RANGITOTO BEYOND

MILFORD BEACH & RANGITOTO
NORTH SHORE, AUCKLAND, N.Z.

'Coming Home' (1993)

I made this
painting during
my last year
of living in Sydney.
I dreamed I came
home in a Waka

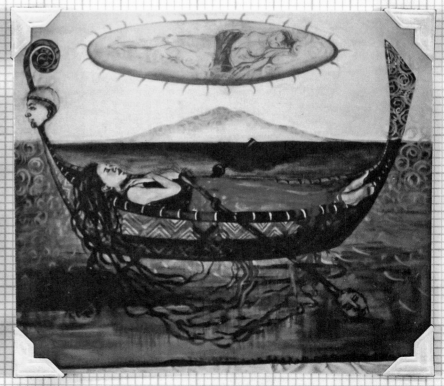

Curried Pumpkin Soup

2 T sunflower oil
1 red onion, finely sliced
1 tsp each of ground coriander, cumin, garam masala, tumeric
1 tsp black mustard seeds
1 litre chicken or vegetable stock
1 butternut pumpkin, peeled, deseeded & diced
1 medium potato, peeled and diced
Salt & Pepper
Saute onion and spices in the oil, add the pumpkin, potato,
and stock, simmer until the vegetables are soft.
Puree with a wand stick.
Serve with a large dollop of natural yogurt, lemon juice, s&p
An exciting addition: drop in fresh scallops, 2-3 mins before serving

Beetroot Salad (leigh)

- Roasted beetroot
- Cooked, chopped bacon
- Toasted hazelnuts (optional)

Mix together.

Onion & garlic - cook in a little oil, add balsamic vinegar, add a fruit juice (2 tbsp ±) & let thicken (the dressing). Throw over beetroot mix, add chopped tomatoes, feta, coriander, mint - Serve - Savour

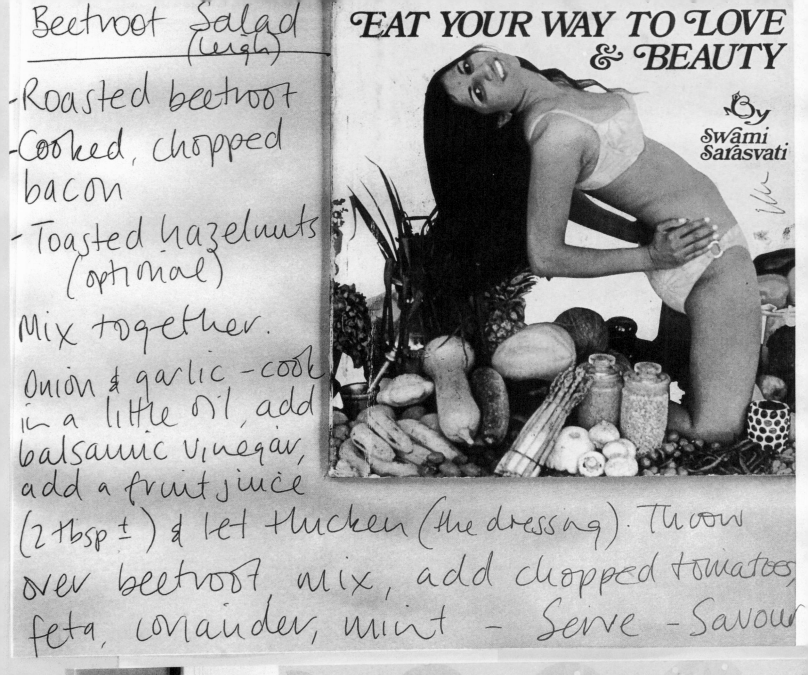

EAT YOUR WAY TO LOVE & BEAUTY

By Swami Sarasvati

Grate 1 big tin of baby beetroots
Add a tub of lite sour cream
Add 2 dessertspoons of masterfoods horseradish cream
Add 1/4 red onion very finely diced
Add salt & pepper
Mix together ....voila

2 Rolls - 1 Metre Each Roll. **Acid and Lignin Free.**

2 Rolls - 1 Metre Each Roll. **Acid and Lignin Free.**

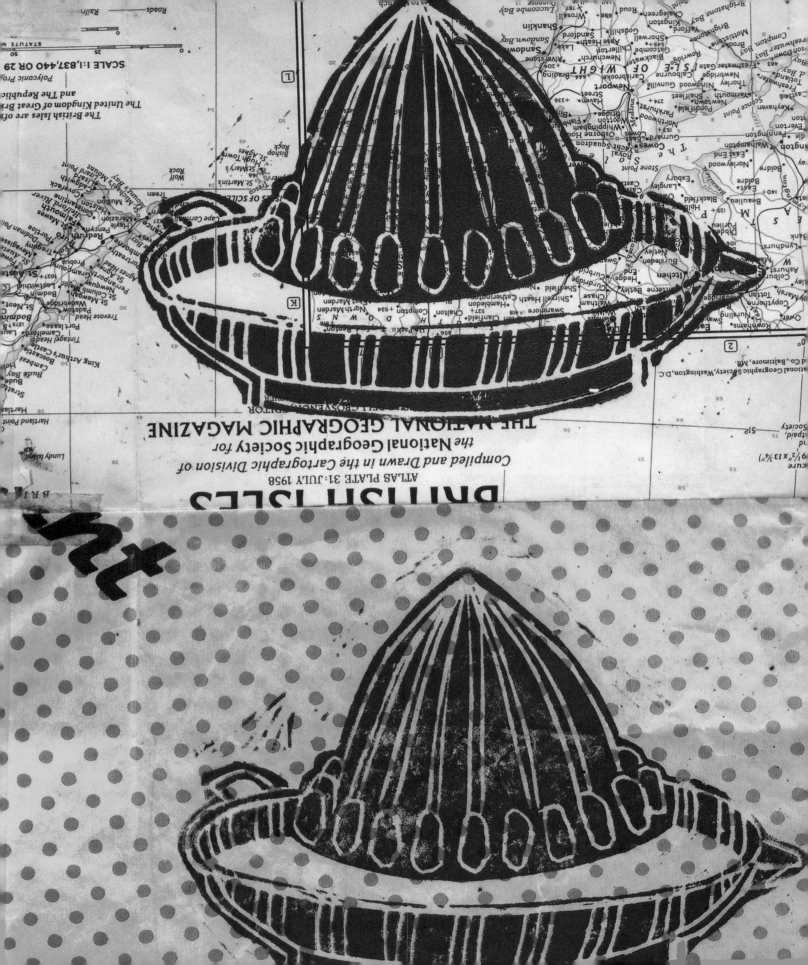

1 alyssa
2 Daniel
3 phillip
4 Rangi
5 Erika
6 Joe

MSV

MANUKAU
SCHOOL
OF
VISUAL
ART

Talks ab
state,
talks about
Ambiguous

Italian Zucchinis (MARY)

Grate long ribbons of
zucchinis Layout on
a wide flat dish.
Marinade with:
3-4 Tblsp Olive oil
juice of 2-3 lemons
sea salt - leave 1 hr.
Sprinkle over-untoasted
pine nuts & shaved parmesan

FARMHOUSE TREATS
BLACKBALLS

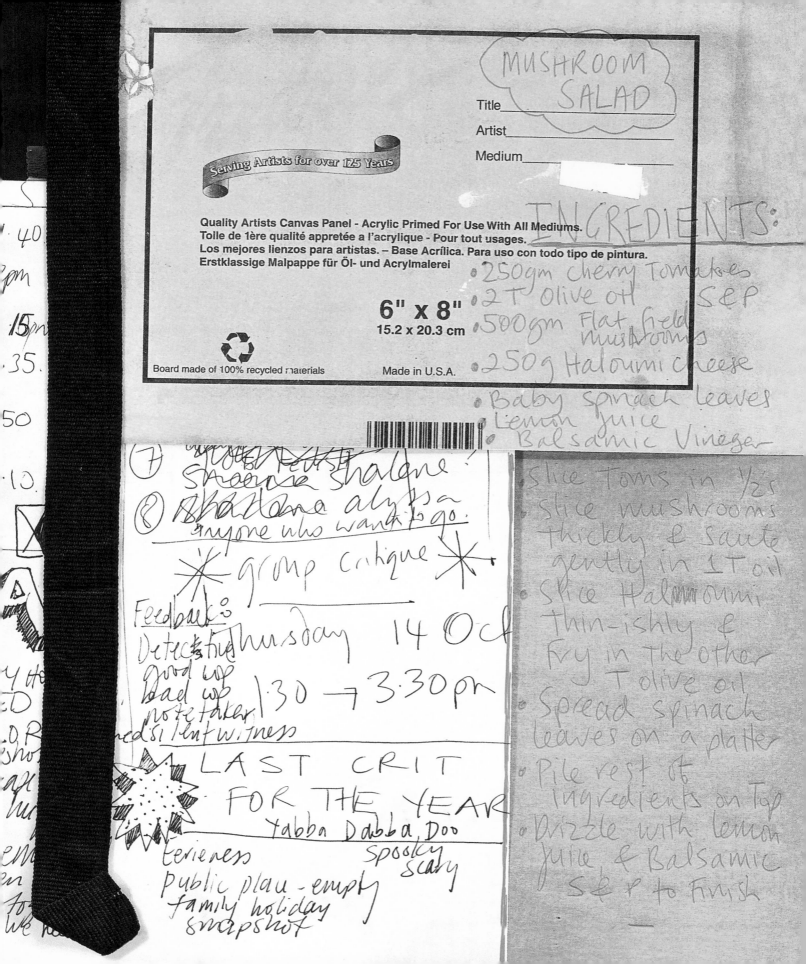

Title _____ MUSHROOM SALAD

Artist _____

Medium _____

Serving Artists for over 125 Years

Quality Artists Canvas Panel - Acrylic Primed For Use With All Mediums.
Toile de 1ère qualité apprêtée a l'acrylique - Pour tout usages.
Los mejores lienzos para artistas. – Base Acrílica. Para uso con todo tipo de pintura.
Erstklassige Malpappe für Öl- und Acrylmalerei

6" x 8"
15.2 x 20.3 cm

Board made of 100% recycled materials   Made in U.S.A.

INGREDIENTS:

- 250gm cherry Tomatoes
- 2T Olive oil   S&P
- 500gm Flat field
    mushrooms
- 250g Haloumi cheese
- Baby spinach leaves
- Lemon juice
- Balsamic Vinegar

- Slice Toms in ½s
- Slice mushrooms
    thickly & saute
    gently in 1T oil
- Slice Haloumi
    thin-ishly &
    Fry in the other
    T olive oil
- Spread spinach
    leaves on a platter
- Pile rest of
    ingredients on Top
- Drizzle with lemon
    Juice & Balsamic
    S&P to Finish

⑦ Sharlene Sharlene!
⑧ Sharlene alysa
    anyone who wants to go.

✴ group critique ✴

Feedback:
Detective Thursday 14 Oct
Good cop
Bad cop   1:30 → 3:30pm
notetaker
Red silent witness

LAST CRIT
FOR THE YEAR
    Yabba Dabba Doo

spooky
scary
eerieness
public place - empty
family holiday
snapshot

WALDORF SALAD

- 2 T Thick cream
- 2 T whole egg mayonnaise
- 1 tsp grain or dijon mustard
- Juice of small lemon. S&P
- 1 cup toasted walnuts.

- 3 apples roughly chopped (skins left on)
- 3 celery sticks - sliced
- 3 spring onions - sliced finely

Mix all ingredients together - serve in lettuce cups.

For a more substantial dish add smoked chicken breast - sliced.

cooking

TIN
SAUCEPAN
SIEVE
LAYER PAN
ROLLING PIN
DOUBLE BOILER
STEAMER
COLANDER
BISCUIT CUTTERS
MEASURING CUP
CASSEROLE
FRYING PAN
PATTY PAN
DRAINING SPOON

most satisfying to see those cakes rise, hear the soup bubbling, and smell the delicious aromas which fill the kitchen.

You should **WASH** your hands and put on your **APRON** before you start. Read the recipe carefully, then set out all the utensils and ingredients required. If the recipe requires the oven to be pre-heated, turn it on before mixing.

WOODEN SPOON
MIXING BOWLS
EGG BEATER
EGG SLICE
SCALES
GRATER
LADLE
SPATULA
WHISK
SCONE TRAY
LOAF TIN

Condensed Milk Salad Dressing

2T condensed milk
1T malt vinegar
2-3 T milk
1tsp mustard
Mix together thoroughly in jar.
Pour over cut salad of:
sliced iceburg lettuce
peeled & sliced cucumbers
sliced tomatoes
quartered hard boiled eggs
    (arrange salad ingredients
in layers, starting with the lettuc
    first, use a glass bowl).

the oven is turned off when the food is cooked.

NIÇOISE salad
serves 6.

6 medium Tomatoes - quartered
6 small potatoes - boiled in
   their skins
3 hard boiled eggs shelled
   and cut into quarters
1 lebanese cucumber
   - peeled and sliced
1 green pepper ⎫ thinly
1 red pepper ⎬ sliced.
6 spring onions - thinly
                    sliced
1 small red onion -
   thinly sliced
1 250gm tin of tuna in
   spring water, drained
   and flaked.
125 gm black olives
12 lettuce leaves, washed
   and pat dry.

Dressing:
6 T olive oil
2 T red wine vinegar
a small handful of
basil leaves - torn.

S. & P.

Spread the lettuce
leaves out on
6 dinner plates
arrange the rest
of the ingredients
artfully on top.
Combine dressing
ingredients in jar
shake and drizzle
over salad.
A great summer dinner!

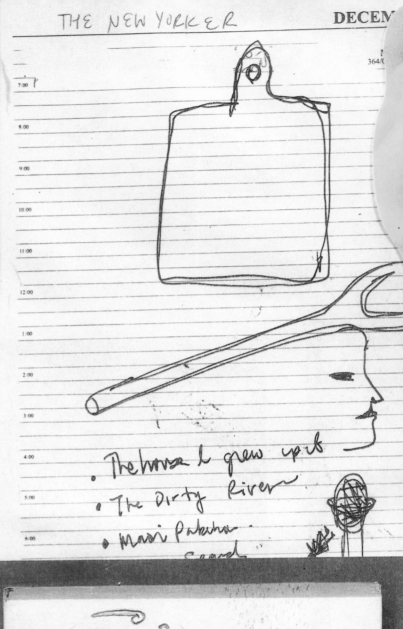

7:00
8:00
9:00
10:00
11:00
12:00
1:00
2:00
3:00
4:00
5:00
6:00

• The house I grew up in
• The Dirty River
• Masi Pakora

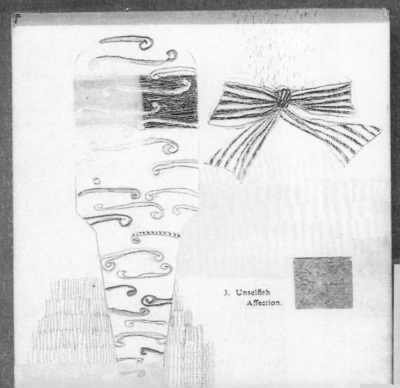

3. Unselfish
   Affection.

Tuna Salad   (Tracey)

1 large (425g) tin Tuna chunks in spring water
1 Lebanese cucumber, peeled and diced
2 tomatoes diced
1 avocado diced
1/2 red onion finely diced
½ small red pepper diced
1 heaped tablespoon whole egg mayonnaise
1 tablespoon chopped parsley
Squeeze of lemon juice
Salt and pepper to taste

Combine ingredients in bowl.
Serve on crackers as finger food
Serve in lettuce cups with crackers as a light lunch
Serve as a dip or salad at a party or BBQ
Popular with kids

Green Salad

Mixed Leaves:
- rocket
- baby spinach
- mesclun
- endive
- fancy lettuce

Blanched green vegetables:
- snow peas
- green beans
- asparagus

Fresh Herbs:
- Italian parsley
- Basil leaves - (torn)
- chives
- coriander

OTHER:
- avo's - sliced & sprinkled with lemon juice
- spring onions
- green capsicums

Method

Assemble all, (or some) of the above in a large salad bowl.

TOSS

Dress just before serving with:

- 2T Olive oil
- 1T Lemon juice
- 2T Red wine vinegar
- 1T Balsamic "
- 1 tsp Honey
- S&P

put into jar + shake.

OPTIONAL EXTRAS:
TOASTED SESAME, SUNFLOWER OR PUMPKIN SEEDS
HANDFUL OF ROASTED CASHEWS ALMONDS OR BRAZILS.

Super Quick Dressing:
- 4 T mayo
- 4 T natural yogurt
- 1 T pesto, S.&P.
- 1 T Lemon juice

ROAST PEAR BEAN AND HAZELNUT SALAD

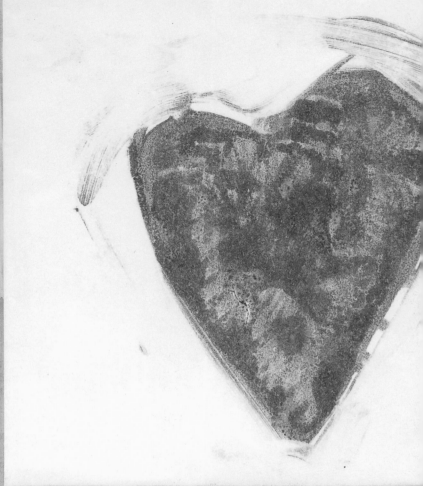

artworks by Joey Fossie

sweet sweet sweet sweet sweet

Dressing:

1 tsp Dijon mustard
2 cloves garlic - finely sliced
2 T red wine vinegar
1 T hazelnut oil
3 T cream

place ingredients into a jar and shake to mix

ROAST PEAR, BEAN & HAZELNUT

Salad: 3 Pears - sliced
500g long green beans
50g hazelnuts —
skinned & chopped.
30g castor sugar
5 T good olive oil.
Sprinkle sugar & oil on pears & beans
Roast, mod oven 15 mins
Toss with nuts & dressing.

POTATO & MUSHROOM

Vegetables

Pickling onions $2.49 lb

Pickled Onions.   (HAZEL)

10 lb. Onions.   3 pts Vinegar.
2 lb Br Sugar.   Allspice.
2 lb Tin Golden Syrup.   Few Cloves.
½ lb Salt   " Chillies.

Ready in about a week.

Bread & Butter Pickle (HAZEL)

4 Medium Onions, 8 cups sliced Telegraph
cucumber, 4 Green Peppers, 1 cup salt, 2 cups
white Vinegar, 2 cups sugar, 2 teaspoons Mustard
seeds, 1 teaspn pickling spice, 2 teaspns turmeric
2 teaspns celery seeds, 4 teaspn ground
cinnamon, 2 Litres water.
  Peel & slice onions, Place cucumber & onion
in large glass bowl, Deseed & slice peppers &
add. Combine Veges & sprinkle with salt, add
cold water, stand for 3hrs, drain thoroughly
without rinsing. In large saucepan combine
vinegar, sugard, Mustard & celery seeds, spice &
tumeric & cinnamon. Heat to boiling add
Veges bring to boiling point again but dont
boil, Pack into hot sterilized jars & seal.

Mandy Thomsett-Taylor

Special Silverbeet/Spinach Feta Pie

Special Spinach & Silverbeet Feta Pie

(Mandy Thompsett Taylor)

Picture a huge steaming golden pie as the centerpiece, a large bottle of HP sauce or a rich tomato chutney nearby, accompanied by a bowlful of honey glazed carrots. This dish has become a family favourite and will easily feed six. It is equally delicious cold, so I always make more than we can eat.

Ingredients:
- 4 sheets ready rolled puff pastry
- 2 blocks of your favourite feta cheese
- 2 cups grated tasty cheese
- 5 eggs beaten with plenty of ground black pepper
- large handful of fresh herbs; basil, thyme, coriander
- 2 large bunches of silverbeet
- 2 large bunches spinach

Method:
Wash silverbeet & spinach in large sinkful of water, wrap in a towel to squeeze out excess water.
Steam or cook the greens till soft, drain well to remove excess liquid. Chop roughly and place in oiled pie dish.
In a bowl, mix eggs and pepper with chopped herbs, crumble in feta. Pour over the top of the greens, help some of the mixture sink through to the bottom with a fork. Cover with a layer of the tasty grated cheese.
Tuck pastry over the top, cutting through the pastry a few times with a sharp knife to let steam escape.
Glaze with beaten egg. Cook mod oven (180 – 200) for about 30 – 40 mins until pastry is golden.

artwork by
Lorraine
Rastorfer

20. June 2004

Hiya Fran,
   Great to catch up, with you this morning.
Thought I'd get this recipe off to you before
I forget. — love Marilyn xx

Kumera & Coconut Curry.

1 tspn curry powder
1 tspn ground cumin
1 tspn garam masala
½ tspn chilli powder
1 Tablespn oil
2 diced onion
1 Tablespn finely chopped ginger
1 teaspn " " garlic
2 large Kumera peeled in chopped into 2cm squares
2 sliced bananas (— add into casserole in last ½ hour)
1 tspn brown sugar
½ tspn salt
¼ cup lemon juice
1 tin coconut milk.
Toasted shredded coconut for garnish.
Heat all spices in oil in pan. Add onion & saute
Add ginger & garlic. and cook. Add Kumera &
toss around. Place in casserole dish (with lid)
and rest of ingredients. Cook for 1-2 hours
at 180°C . Add banana in last ½ hour.
   Garnish with shredded coconut.

RISOTTO (classic) (Penny Coss)

Ingredients: (for four people)

1 cup Arborio rice
2 cups chicken stock
1 cup white wine
1 onion – finely diced
fresh parmesan cheese
2 Tblesp olive oil

Method:
Saute the onion in olive oil in medium sized saucepan
until clear. Put aside using a slotted spoon.
Pour rice into pot with oil
Cook until rice is coated with the oil and a little
transparent, about 5 minutes.
Mix stock with wine and heat gently in separate pot.
Slowly add ½ cup of this mix at a time, to the rice,
stirring all the while until the rice is cooked. This
takes some time, wait for the liquid to evaporate each
time before you add more. For a really creamy risotto,
stir more constantly. Add in onion and then parmesan just
before serving.

Suggestions for risotto variations:

-Fresh asparagus and parmesan
-Spinach, salmon & sundried tomato
-Zucchini, lemon, parmesan and toasted pinenuts
-Chicken, tomatoes, parmesan & fresh basil
-pumpkin and feta
-mushrooms, parsley and parmesan
-prawns, dill and lemon

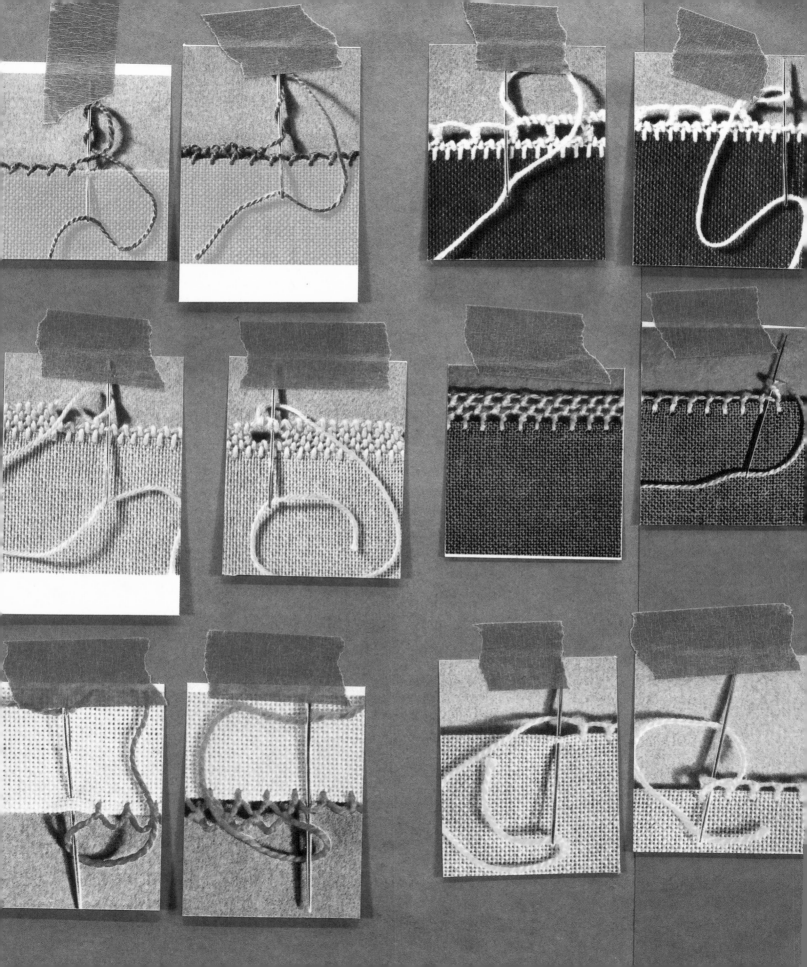

Cauliflower & Pinenut Noodle Bowl

Serves 4

1 Whole cauliflower broken into small pieces and steamed
2 cloves garlic, finely sliced
Heaps of chopped parsley, at least ½ cup
2 Tblesp butter
dash olive oil
½ cup crumbled feta
skinny spaghetti noodles cooked until al dente
toasted pinenuts. 1½ cup
s&p to taste
1 cup cherry tomatoes, halved
XXXXX
Method
Saute garlic in butter & olive oil until just beginning to turn
slightly golden add parsley and plenty of S&P
Add hot steamed cauliflower mash roughly with fork.
Place noodles into individual bowls.
Spoon over cauliflower mix
Sprinkle feta pinenuts and cherry toms on top
Optional Extras or replacement ingredients:
coriander
red capsicum
chives
basil

This dish is one of my all time
favourites. It is fresh and tasty right down
to the last noodle. It makes a very delicious
and satisfying healthy meal

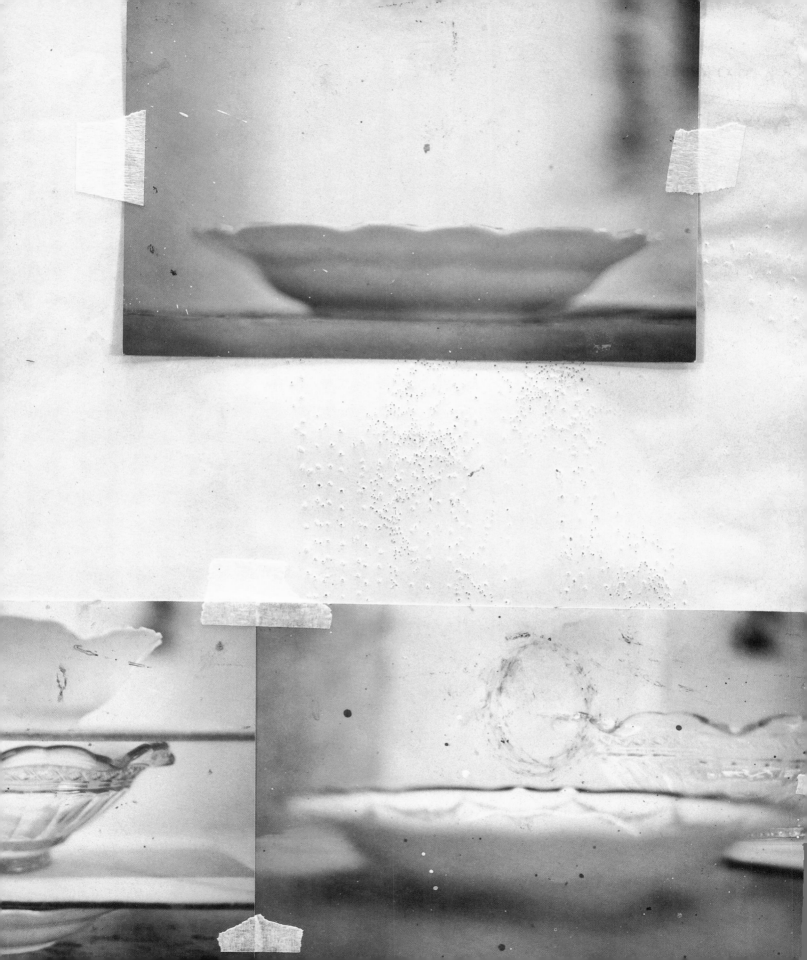

Spinach + Gruyere Fritters

250g frozen spinach (thawed and then squeeze out excess juice)

1 cup cold mashed potato

100g gruyere cheese grated

2 spring onions, sliced finely

2 Tbsp self raising flour

3 eggs, beaten

1/4 tsp each: salt, nutmeg + pepper

- chop spinach roughly
- mix all ingredients together
- cook 2-3 minutes each side.

NB put mixture in fridge for an hour. before frying-helps fritter to stick together

handy hint:
It is always helpful to have a couple of packs of frozen spinach in the freezer. Takes up less room and tastes just as great as fresh stuff.

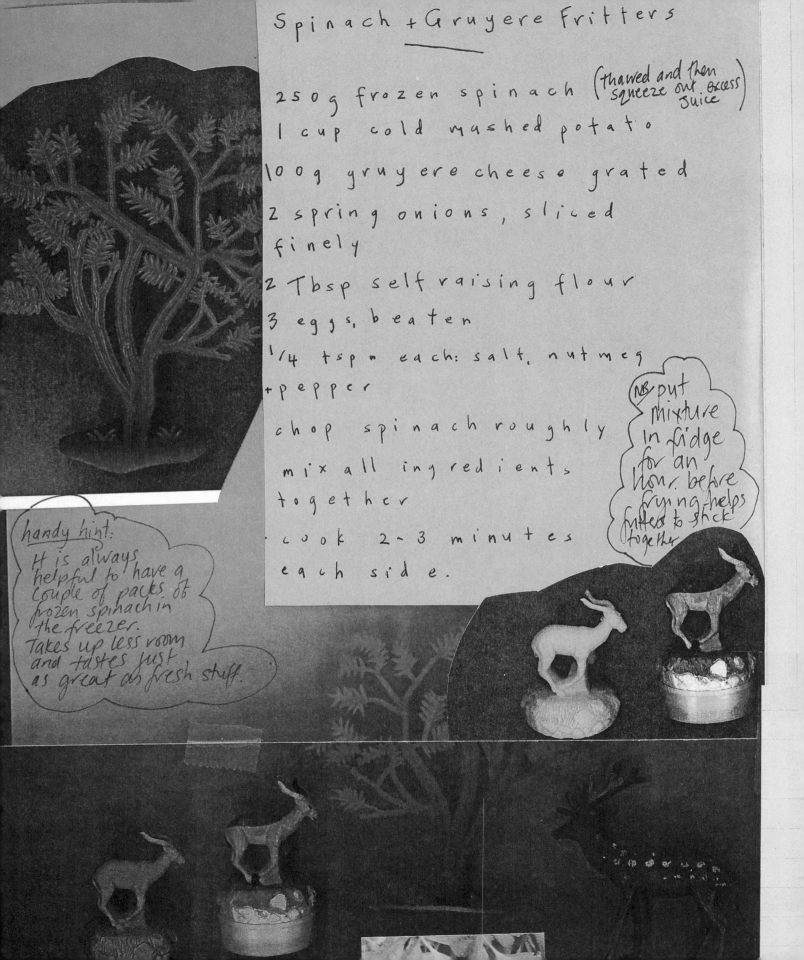

Spicy Pumpkin Fritters

- 250 g raw pumpkin
- 1/2 red onion
- 1/4 cup self raising flour
- 2 eggs
- 3 Tbspns favourite spice paste
- rind - grated - + juice one lime

grate pumpkin
mix together all ingredients
fry large spoonfuls 5 min each side
serve with yoghurt + mint
or tomato chutney/relish
+ green salad
(could use parsnips, spring onion + kumera)

Zucchini, Pea & Feta FRITTERS

3 grated zucchinis
2 Beaten eggs
1/2 block Feta (crumbled)
1 cup baby peas (cooked)
1 T plain flour (S+P)
optional - a big handful of fresh spinach leaves
Mix above ingredients tog.
fry in a mix of olive oil & butter (2T of each)
Serve with chopped coriander, tomato salsa, chilli sauce.

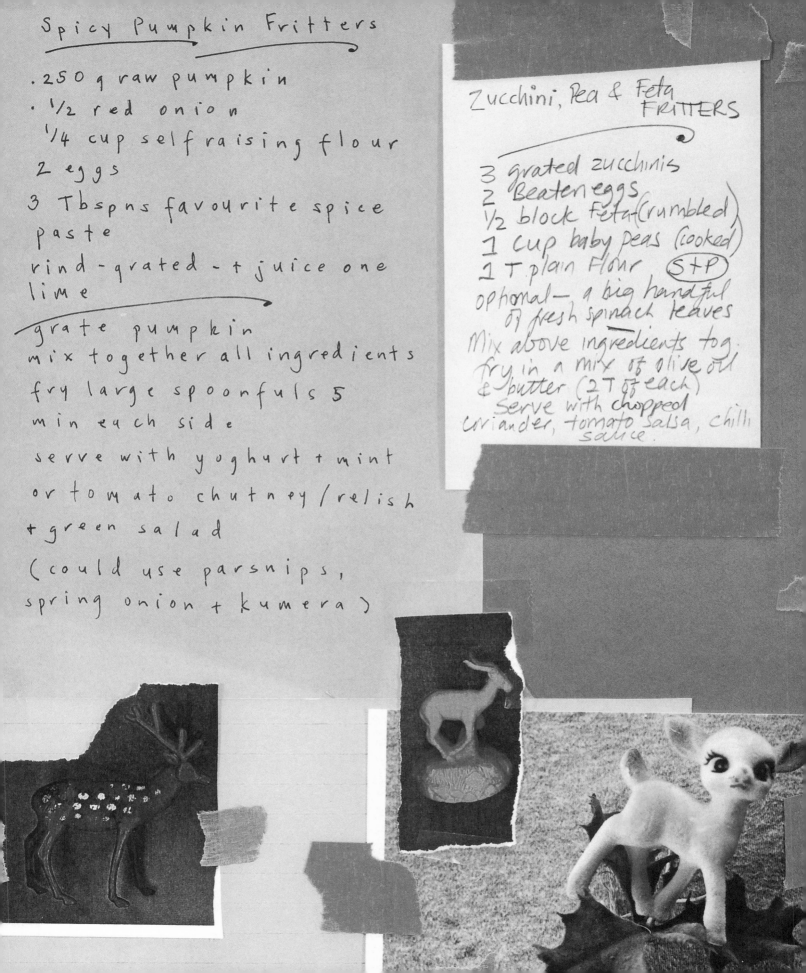

CREAMED SPINACH

This dish is so great as it is firstly, very healthy, goes with many
different dishes as a side and is a fantastic colour and texture. I
often eat this with crumbed fish or roast chicken and rice. Just
note, spinach reduces down a lot when cooked so you need to start
with a lot.

Ingredients:
2 large bunches spinach (frozen packets are fine, use 2)
1 finely diced onion
1 tblesp olive oil
¾ cup cream (I use lite)
salt & pepper

Method:
Steam the spinach for 3-5 mins.
Meanwhile saute the onion in olive oil in med. sized saucepan until
transparent. Transfer spinach in with the onion, pour in the cream
and bring to a simmer. Blend roughly with a wand blender, right there
in the saucepan. Season with plenty of S& P. Simmer away for about 10
mins until the cream is absorbed and the spinach is a nice
consistency, a soft custard.

Optional extra:
Add 1 cup of frozen peas with the spinach, whilst steaming.

NOTES:

New Zealand
KOWHAI
MT. COOK
BELLBIRD
CAPE REINGA
KAITAIA
RUSSELL
PAIHIA
WHAN
AKA
AUCKLAND

ANNIVERSARIES

First	Paper
Second	Cotton
Third	
Third	Leather
Fourth.........	Books or Plants
Fifth.........	Wood
Sixth	Iron
Seventh	Copper or brass
Eighth.........	Pottery
Ninth	Wool
Tenth.........	Tin or Aluminium
Eleventh	Steel
Twelfth.......	Silk or Linen
Thirteenth.....	Lace
Fourteenth	Ivory (or plastic)
Fifteenth	~~Crystal~~ Crystal
Twentieth	China
Twenty-fifth	Silver
Thirtieth......	Pearl
Fortieth Fortieth	Ruby
Forty-fifth	Sapphire
FIFTIETH........	**GOLDEN**
Fifty-fifth	Emerald
Sixtieth.........	**DIAMOND**

CORN FRITTERS
1 can creamed corn
1 egg beaten
2 T flour
s&p
Mix all ingredients
together with a fork.
Drop spoonful lots
into sizzling butter
in frypan. Flip after a
couple of minutes.
Serve with salsa,
sour cream, bacon,
chopped coriander,
sweet chilli sauce
guacamole etc.....

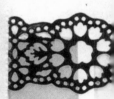

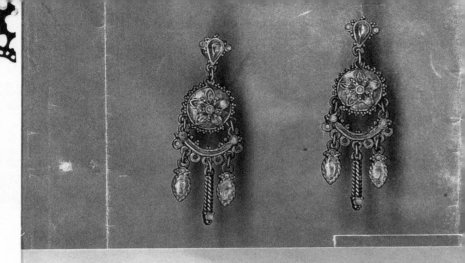

Corn savouries

BREAD CASES:
18 slices thin bread
Butter

FILLING:
1 rasher bacon
1 onion
1 x 310 g tin creamed corn
1 tablespoon milk
½ cup grated cheese
Freshly ground pepper
2 tablespoons chopped parsley

BREAD CASES: Remove crusts from bread slices. Butter bread.

Cut into rounds, using a 7 cm pastry-cutter, or into 8 cm squares. Place butter side down in patty tins.

Bake at 180 degrees C for 15 to 20 minutes or till golden brown.

Remove from patty tins and keep hot.

FILLING: Remove rind from bacon. Chop bacon finely. Peel and finely chop onion.

In a saucepan cook bacon and onion till tender. Add corn, milk, cheese, pepper and parsley.

Cook for 3 to 4 minutes. Spoon hot mixture into hot breadcases.

Have stay-hot tray heating and place hot savouries on top to keep warm.

Makes 18.

Spicy Brown lentils & Tomatoes

This dish is a lovely warming winter dish that is made easy by being cooked all in one oven dish.

Ingredients:
1 finely diced red onion
2 cloves garlic, crushed
2 red birdseye chillis, finely sliced, (deseeded if you want a milder dish)
2 tblesp olive oil
1 can brown lentils, (these are surprisingly good-experiment with different brands to discover which ones you like the best).
2 sticks celery, finely sliced on an angle
2 cups vegetable stock
2 Tblesp tamari
1 carrot, peeled and finely sliced
1 lg potato peeled and diced
2 cans Italian tomatoes
2 Tblesp tomato paste
splash red wine
salt & pepper
handful of fresh herbs such as:
oregano, thyme, parsley
optional Extra:
1 large bunch steamed spinach, drained

Method:
Saute the onion, garlic and chilli, in olive oil, cook for a few mins. Transfer to baking dish, strain and rinse lentils, add to dish, add all other ingredients.
Bake 45 mins in moderate oven.

Non vegetarian Optional extra:
Slice in some spicy chorizo, or even left over BBQ sausages about 30 mins into cooking.

HOW TO MAKE A WOOLLY BALL

Fig. 2 shows clearly how to start making a woolly ball. One colour, or several different co... may be used. Older children can get good effects by making each round a different colo... that the finished ball is striped. If the child makes the ball for a young brother or sister, le... tie it with elastic, leaving a long end which can be fastened to baby's pram. This ma... splendid plaything.

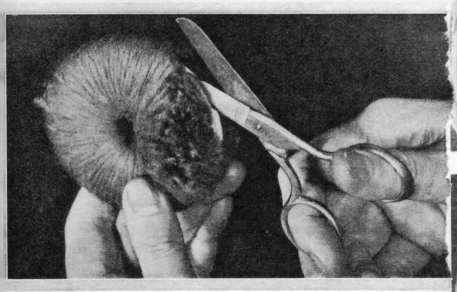

In Fig. 3 it can be seen how the woolly ball is cut. The space between the cardboard, wher... string to tie the ball goes, is also seen. Two yellow balls make a chicken. The legs (a pi... millinery wire, bound with yellow wool, with the toes separate) are inserted through th... in the larger ball before the wool is cut, and the smaller ball is attached for the head. A... and ink spots form beak and eyes.

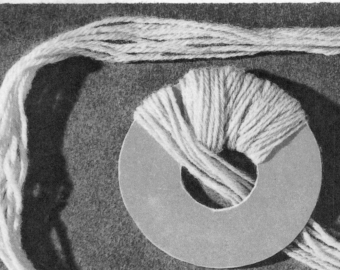

▲ Winding the yarn onto the frame ▼ The finished pompo...

Cauliflower & Cheese Sauce Filo Baskets   makes 12

1 cauliflower broken into florets and steamed
24 sheets filo pastry
cheese sauce, (see below)
chopped Italian parsley
toasted cashew nuts
3-4 Tblesp melted butter

Grease a tray of large patty pans, (the ones you make the large muffins in) or even better the silicone ones. Push in 2 sheets of filo, brushing with melted butter inbetween the two sheets first, to make a 'nest'. Spoon in steamed florets, spoon over sauce, bake in moderate oven till pastry is golden brown, (about 10 - 15 mins) Sprinkle with parsley and toasted cashews.

Cheese Sauce

2Tblesp Butter
3 Tblesp Flour
2 ½ cups milk, 1 ½ cups grated tasty cheese
ground black pepper

Melt the butter in a pan. Add the flour a little at a time, mixing well after each addition, until the mixture binds together. Continue stirring and cook for 2-3 minutes. Keep stirring and add the milk a little at a time mixing well to ensure no lumps are formed. Add in cheese, return to a low heat and bring to the boil gradually, stirring continuously, until the sauce has thickened.
Season with the pepper.

Vegetable Crepes With Cheese Sauce   (Jo)
Crepes:

2 eggs
1 cup white high grade flour
1&1/4 cup milk
2 Tblesp vegetable oil or 2 Tblesp milk
pinch of salt

Blend above ingredients really well with a whisk, refrigerate whilst preparing the mashed vegetables. The consistency of the mixture should be like pouring cream. Heat a nonstick pan sprayed with a little oil, pour in about 1/4 cup of the batter and swirl around the pan, flip when when slightly browned on bottom side, you will need to lift up corner of crepe to check. This mix should make about 10 crepes.
Nb. you can use wholemeal flour if you want a heavier dish.

Mashed vegetables:

Steam a mix of broccoli, potato, kumera (or sweet potato), zucchini & carrot. Mash together with 1 Tblesp butter, a little milk and plenty of salt & pepper.

To assemble:

Place a large spoonful of vegetable mixture in the centre of a crepe, smooth out with fingers to a long sausage like shape, roll up and place in baking dish, repeat until all crepes are filled. Pour cheese sauce (see above) over these and top with tomato slices and more grated tasty cheese, bake 20 mins. Serve with green salad.

Roast Vegetable & Chickpea Bake

Ingredients:
½ Butternut pumpkin - skin off & cut into chunks
3 medium sized zucchinis – halved lengthways and sliced thickly on the diagonal
2 red peppers – deseeded and sliced thickly
6 cloves garlic, slightly squashed, don't bother skinning completely
6 small pickling onions, cut into halves lengthways, once again, don't bother peeling completely
1tsp cumin seeds
1tsp coriander seeds
2T olive oil
plenty salt & pepper

Baby spinach leaves for platter bed

Garnish:
½ block feta – crumbled
1 punnet cherry tomatoes - halved
1 large bunch fresh coriander – chopped roughly

Dressing:
Balsamic Vinegar
Avocado or lime infused oil or good olive oil

Method:
Toss vegetables in olive oil, put into large flat oven tray
Roast for 30 mins in moderate oven, turning once
Scrape out onto a bed of baby spinach leaves that have been well rinsed and spread over a serving platter
Sprinkle garnish ingredients over and lastly dressings
Best eaten whilst still warm

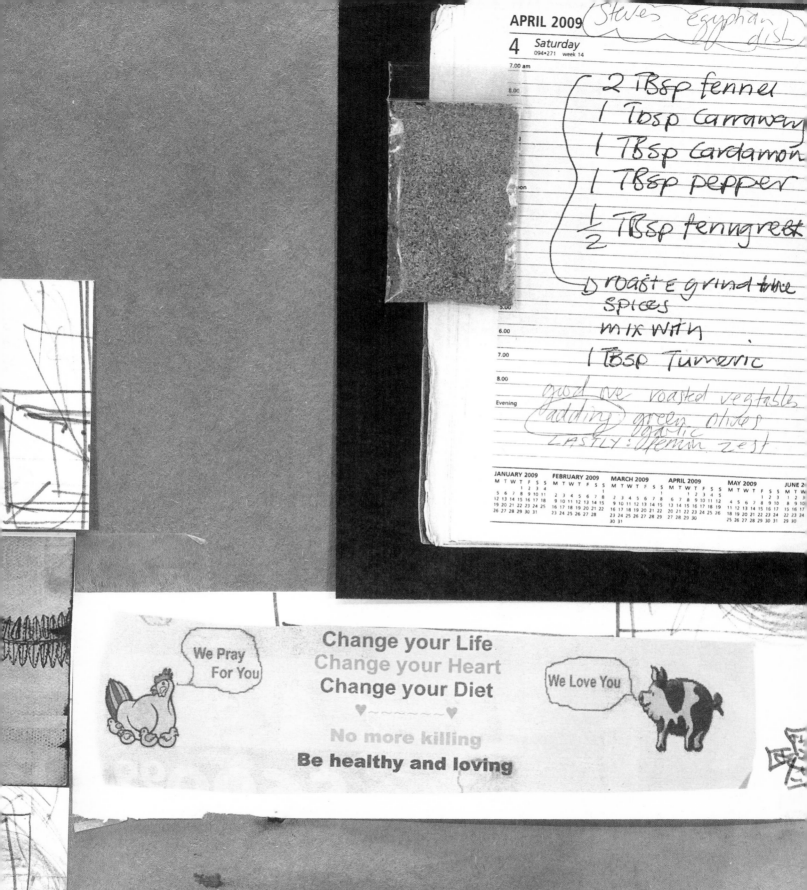

SCALLOPED POTATOES

5-6 large potatoes
1 clove garlic
2-3T butter
1 cup milk
1/2 cup milk cream
1/2 tsp grated nutmeg, fresh
2/3 cup grated cheese
salt & pepper

Peel potatoes and slice thinly.
Rub the baking dish with the garlic
and butter generously.
Arrange potato slices in layers in
shallow baking dish.
Scald milk, add nutmeg, S & P.
Pour over potatoes, sprinkle
with cheese and dot with some of
the butter.
Bake in mod oven 40 - 50 mins until potatoes
are golden and tender.
Serves 6

Notes:	Sadie, Bede, fran, Tom Avondale NZ	000656 04/09/07

名花牌

发夹

中国 上海

TRADE MARK *Flower Brand* HAIR GRIPS SHANGHAI

Gado Gado

This dish is a mix of raw and cooked vegetables served with a mildly spicy sauce. A healthy summer feast.

Peanut Sauce
1 onion — finely diced
1 thumbsize piece of fresh ginger, finely grated, skin & all
1 small red birdseye chilli, deseeded & finely sliced
1 tsp honey
1 T soy sauce
3 T natural peanut butter (you can buy this from health food shops)
2-3 bay leaves
juice of 1 lemon
1 cup water

Saute first 3 ingredients for a few minutes until onion is soft and transparent.
Add the remaining ingredients and simmer for 5-10 mins until sauce thickens, season with plenty of salt & pepper. You may need to thin the sauce with a little more water.

Pour the sauce (hot) over an artful arrangement of the following ingredients:

Steamed cauliflower, broccoli & carrots
Boiled baby potatoes
Crunchy bean sprouts
Quartered hard boiled eggs
Iceberg lettuce leaves
Sliced & partially skinned cucumber

Nb. This works best if you plate up individually. Also prawn crackers brought from your local Chinese are great on the side. You can buy these from asian supermarkets and cook you own, good fun to watch these expand rapidly in hot oil.

Californian Omlette   (serves 2)   (megan)

Ingredients:

1T butter
4 eggs, beaten lightly
Salt & Pepper
1 avocado
1 handful of alfalfa sprouts
2 T cream cheese

Method:
Melt butter in omlette pan, over medium
heat, pour eggs into sizzling butter.
Gently scrape bottom of pan moving cooked
egg towards centre, a few times.
When egg is nearly set spread avocado,
cream cheese and sprouts over half of the
omlette. Season with plenty of S & P.
Flip other half on top, cut in half and
transfer onto two plates.
Serve with grilled herby tomatoes, and hash
browns.

Herbed tomatoes:
Slice lg toms in half, sprinkle with a mix
of chopped fresh herbs such as parsley,
coriander & oregano, S&P, put under grill
for 10- 15 mins.

Potato Rosti:
Grate two potatoes, squeeze out liquid
mix in 1 beaten egg, season with S&P.
Fry in spoonful lots in heavy frypan,
flipping over and cooking until golden
brown, potato is soft and edges crispy.
Good with steamed spinach or pesto.

KUMERA, RED ONION & ZUCCHINI BAKE

2 - 3 kumera - peeled & sliced thinly
2 red onions - large, sliced thinly into rounds
3, lg zucchini sliced in rounds, on an angle (angle)
250 ml pouring cream
250 ml milk   Salt & pepper
2 T butter   small handful fresh thyme leaves
Oil a roasting pan, stack alternate handfuls of
kumera, onion & zucchini in rows along the pan,
leaning at a slight angle.
Pour the milk and cream over. Sprinkle the thyme,
dot the butter and season well with S&P.
Roast 45 mins, mod oven. Top should be crispy brown
and bottom moist, creamy and soft.

This is the first &
only kete I have
woven. My friend
Dr tti has
this now.

TIKA
(the right (the right way)
BY BEDE W. Way)

inner mostness

I draw this
in sydney
thinking of
TE AROHA

my
girlfriends
gave me
this
special
girl
when I
left NZ
In 1979.
I still
have
her safe
& sound
←

RUSSIAN VEGETABLE PIE

Pastry Crust.

2C Plain flour
pinch salt
2T butter
a little iced water
— rub butter into flour & salt
make a well, slowly add a
little water, mixing with a
bread knife.
Form into a ball, roll out ½
on floured board then place
into bottom of greased pie dish
Bake for 10mins, moderate
oven, until beginning to
brown & puff slightly.

Filling

250gm cream cheese
spread over warm base
4 hard boiled eggs - sliced
½ red cabbage - sliced thinly
1 onion diced - small
handful of fresh mixed herbs
thyme, sage, oregano etc,

To assemble.

Place eggs on top of cream
cheese, then cabbage mixture.
Roll out rest of dough and
make lid for pie. Brush with milk.
Bake in moderate oven
for 30 mins.

simple yet effective knitted belt with woven bows worked to match the colour of the dress.

...ver belt with ...ven bows

...it 26–28in waist.
...every additional inch
...ired, add 6sts to the total
...n.

3in wide, satin or taffeta
Waist length stiffening 2½in
wide

Belt

Using No.8 needles and A,
cast on 151sts.
Beg with a K row work 21
rows st st.
Place marker thread round
central st to mark centre back
of Belt. Cast off.

st and 1 row below cast off
edge. Pass yarn under centre
st 5 rows below cast off edge
and insert needle from front to
back of work in centre of st
3sts to the left of centre st
and 1 row below cast off
edge. Bring needle from back
to front 1 row below last st
to right of central st and pass
through centre st, then insert
needle into centre of st below
last st to left of central st
taking the needle through to

group to the left of first group.
Continue in this way to left
hand edge of belt, then work
right hand to correspond.

To make up

Cut stiffening to same size as
Belt. Cut lining, allowing ½in
turnings all round. Tack
stiffening to Belt and cover
with lining, turning in edges
and sewing securely around
all edges. Cover 4 rings with

Bill & Jules

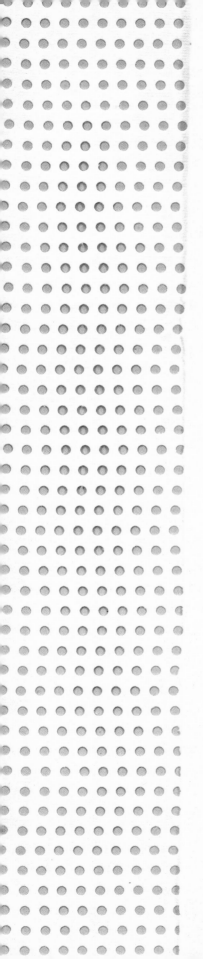

Egg Foo Yung

My stepfather was not the greatest in the kitchen in fact apart from this dish only thing I ever saw him do was roast peanuts.
I taught him how to slice a mango and he really took that on board and became quite the expert.
This first recipe is for a very simplified version of the Chinese classic. The second recipe is a little more sophisticated.

Egg Foo **Yung** (Billy Wood Style)

6 eggs beaten, with salt and pepper
1 large handful of toasted cashews
1 cup cooked peas
1 handful bean sprouts
½ onion finely sliced
3 rashers bacon, finely sliced, *& fried in own fat first.* *(- non veg option)*
1T olive oil
dash soy sauce.

Method:
Cook as you would an omlette.
Sauté onion first, remove from pan, pour in eggs, lift edges towards centre, when nearly cooked sprinkle in other ingredients, adding in onion as well, flip over sections, briefly,
Serve immediately.

egg foo yung (fancy style)

Omlette:
Same as above, taking out the soy sauce and adding in any or all of the following:
sliced fresh mushrooms
red peppers, sliced
spring onions, sliced
shrimp (small prawns). (non veg option)
Sauce
1 cup vegetable stock
1 T oyster sauce
1T soy sauce
Bring above ingredients to the boil, thicken with:
1T cornflour dissolved in 4T water.
Pour sauce over cooked omlette just before serving

3$ 5.00

vegetable burgers

mashed vegetable burgers

Mashed Vegetable Burgers

3 cups of mashed vegetables -use a mix of:
potato, kumera, sweet potato, carrots, broccoli,
swede, parsnips, peas.
Steam, then mash with a knob of butter and S&P.
Beat an egg and stir into mixture, when cooled,
refrigerate further to allow for better handling.
Shape into patties with floured hands. Egg and
breadcrumb. Sprinkle with sesame seeds and
sunflower seeds, bake on oven tray, moderate
oven 30 mins, or until golden and turning crispish
on outside.
Serve in toasted burger buns with beetroot, tomato,
lettuce and maybe melted cheese, mayo or chutney.

Spinach & Rice Burgers

1 large bunch fresh spinach, steamed and drained
of all juices. Alternatively use frozen spinach thawed,
heated and all juice squeezed out
1 large mashed potato
2 cups cooked rice
1 smallish red onion finely diced
1 large bunch fresh coriander, finely chopped
1 egg, beaten
Mix above ingredients, shape into patties,
egg and breadcrumb.
Sprinkle pumpkin seeds on top.
Bake on oven tray, serve in toasted pita with slices of
tomato or spicy chutney

soyabean Burgers

1 cup soyabeans, soaked, drained, boiled with fresh
water and drained again. OR use canned soyabeans. Mash beans
roughly with potato masher or use a wand stick.
I Tblesp tahini
2 cups mashed cooked pumpkin
3 spring onions finely sliced
1 egg, beaten
½ tsp ground garum masala
1 tsp ground cumin
1 tsp ground coriander
Mix ingredients together, make patties,
egg & breadcrumb,
bake 20 mins, moderate oven.
Serve with lettuce tomato, alfalfa and mayo in ciabatta rolls.

soya beans

SOYA
soyabeans
SOYA

S

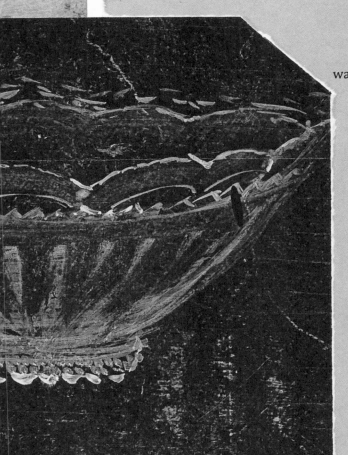

NOTES:

Plate 3

ALBATROSSES IN FLIGHT

Honey, Garlic + Green Beans with
<u>Toasted almonds:</u>

1 lg handful fresh green beans
1 lg " of raw almonds
2 teaspoons honey
2 cloves garlic (thinly sliced)
1 T Butter
1 T Olive oil
• Blanch beans then revive
under cold tap. Toast almonds
in fry pan (after you have sliced
them chunkily)
• Saute garlic in butter & oil.
add in honey, heat & mix.
• Pour this mix over beans
& almonds.
     Serve.

Vegetable Lasagne

Ingredients:
Lasagne Pasta, you can use either the instant flat sheets or a packet of dried ribboned pasta that has the curled edges.
I prefer to cook the lasagne pasta rather than use the instant as I think it taste better, however if you are in a hurry go the instant! Cook Pasta in a large pot of water until just al dente, be careful not to over cook as it will go mushy.

Butternut pumpkin - 1 small one, skinned, deseeded and sliced
Spinach - either a large bunch steamed or use a packet of
                frozen stuff.
Ricotta - 500gms
Tasty cheese - 2 cups grated
Parmesan - 1 cup finely grated
2 Tblesp olive oil
2 cloves garlic
Onion - 1 large or 2 smaller, finely diced
Italian Tomatoes - 2 cans
Tomato Paste - 2 Tblesp
Fresh herbs - mix of oregano, coriander, little bit of thyme
Salt & Pepper

Tomato Sauce - sauté garlic & onion in the olive oil, taking care to not brown the garlic. When onion is transparent add the cans of tomatoes, tomato paste, herbs and s&p to taste. Simmering for about 10 mins, reduce the liquid a little, if you have used cans of whole tomatoes you will need to mash them up a both with a wand stick, easier to use crushed toms.

To Assemble:
Place 1/2 cup of the sauce on bottom of baking dish, layer ingredients in following order:
Pasta, spinach, pumpkin, tomato sauce, cheeses
Aim to make about 3 layers of each finishing with grated tasty cheese on top.

325°F, for one hour.

PESTO

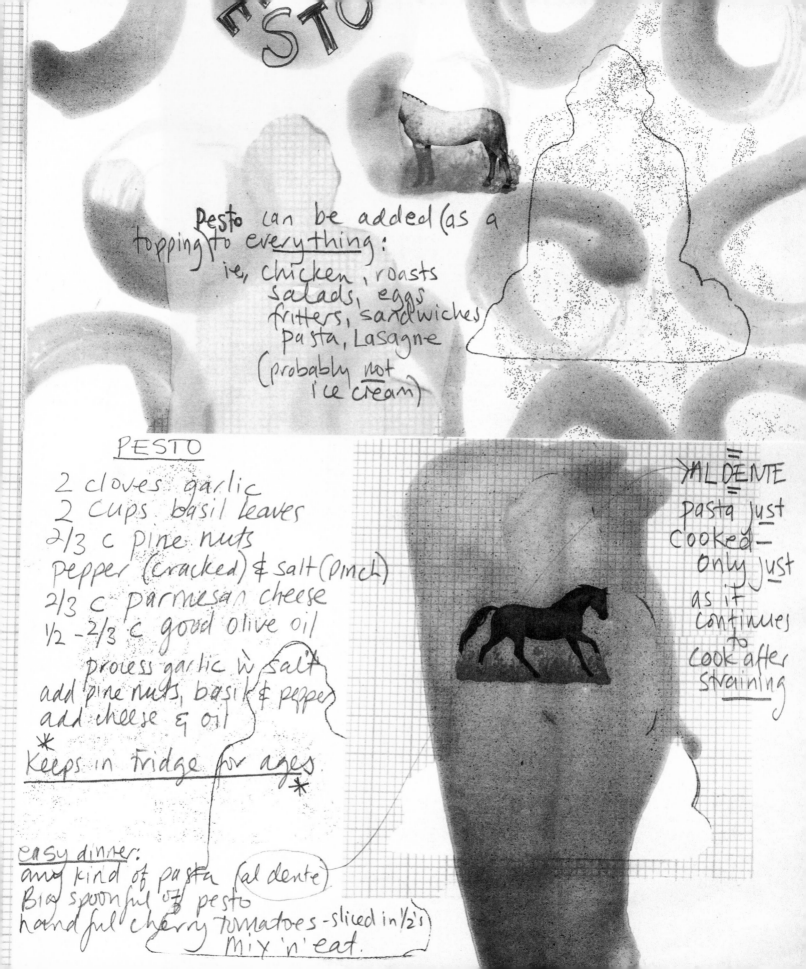

Pesto can be added (as a topping) to everything:
ie, chicken, roasts
salads, eggs
fritters, sandwiches
pasta, Lasagne
(probably not
ice cream)

PESTO

2 cloves garlic
2 cups basil leaves
2/3 c pine nuts
pepper (cracked) & salt (pinch)
2/3 c parmesan cheese
½ - 2/3 c good olive oil

process garlic w salt
add pine nuts, basil & pepper
add cheese & oil
*
Keeps in fridge for ages.
*

easy dinner:
any kind of pasta (al dente)
Big spoonful of pesto
handful cherry tomatoes - sliced in ½'s
Mix 'n' eat.

AL DENTE
pasta just
cooked -
Only just
as it
continues
to
cook after
straining

per cent iodine solution or other mild antiseptic applied around the edge of the blister. Cover with a sterile dressing.

CUTS, SCRATCHES, ABRASIONS

To avoid infection wash your hands before treating any injury. Using sterile gauze, clean the skin around the wound with soap and running tap water, washing *away* from the wound. Apply a mild antiseptic and cover with a sterile gauze.

There is always the danger of tetanus (lockjaw) particularly in deep or dirty wounds. A reddened, hot, painful area around the wound, red streaks, radiating up the arm or leg and chills or fever are signs of infection and may not appear for several days. If they do, see a doctor without delay.

DISLOCATION

Do not attempt to move or set the joint. Get the patient to a doctor or hospital as quickly as possible. If he cannot be moved (as with a dislocated hip) call a doctor.

SUNBURN

If the skin is reddened but not blistered, apply cold cream or mineral oil. Do *not* use butter or margarine; they may introduce infection. If the skin is blistered or extensively burnt, cover it with a sterile dressing wet with a weak solution of baking soda (two tablespoonsful to a quart of water). Don't use greasy ointments. Don't re-expose burnt skin until healing is complete. Severe or extensive sunburn requires prompt medical aid.

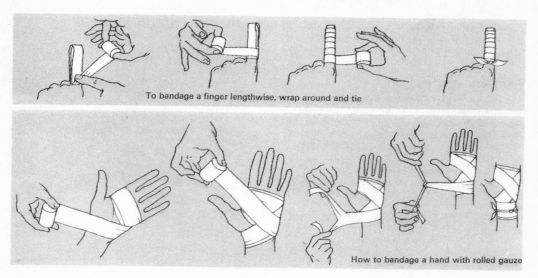

To bandage a finger lengthwise, wrap around and tie

How to bandage a hand with rolled gauze

STUFFED POTATOES (and toppings)

Classic
• Parsley, onion & grated cheese.
Bake potatoes in a reasonably hot oven for 45 mins.
Scrape out insides leaving a thin layer of potato
next to the cooked skin. Mash potato with butter,
s & p and a bit of milk. No lumps! Add in grated
cheese, finely chopped parsley and very finely diced
onion. Stuff back into their shells. bake another
10 mins until cheese is melted and mixture is turning
golden brown on top.
Other variations:
• Top baked potato, (after you have cut a deep cross
in the top and squeezed up some of the cooked interior)
with a knob of butter, s & p, hot baked beans and
a poached egg.
• Mushrooms, sourcream & chives - saute mushrooms first,
stir in sourcream, snip in chives. Make a deep cross
cross as above and spoon mushroom mixture over.

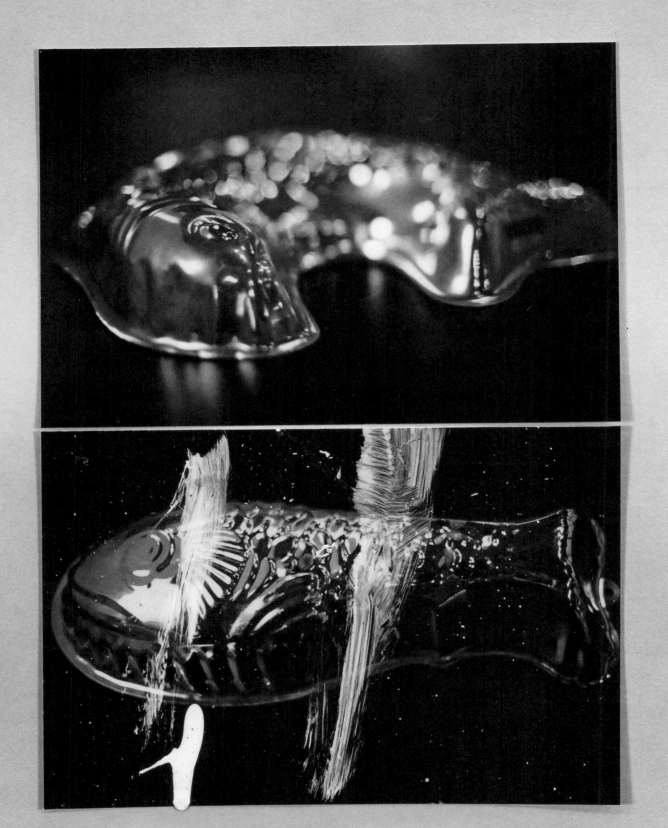

CRUNCHY SALMON PIE

CRUNCHY SALMON PIE (Tracey)

Ingredients:

1½ cups flour
1 cup cheese, grated
½ tsp paprika   pepper & salt
125 g butter
1 x 450 g salmon (canned is fine)
3 eggs, beaten
1 x 250 ml carton sour cream
½ cup cheese grated
1 onion, finely diced
¼ tsp dill
tabasco sauce (optional)

METHOD:

1. Mix first 3 ingredients together
   rub in butter
2. Reserve ½ the mixture, press remainder
   onto base & sides of a 25cm pie dish
3. Drain & flake fish, arrange in dish
4. Combine eggs with remaining ingreds.
5. Pour over salmon, sprinkle with
   remaining crumbs.

BAKE 200.c 35-40 mins
Stand for 10 mins
before before
cutting.

Baked Salmon:

Use fresh salmon steaks or a large fillet that you can cut into smaller slices.
Oil a baking dish and place salmon pieces skin side down.
SPRINKLE over the top:
juice & zest of a lemon and a lime.
2 Tblsp soy sauce or Tamari
plenty salt & pepper
chopped spring onions
cherry tomatoes
Bake
20 mins
moderate oven.

To finish:
add more lime juice
+ sprinkle with fresh chopped coriander
serve with steamed rice & zucchini fritters.

Quick Fish Curry

1 small onion, diced
1 T finely sliced fresh lemongrass
2 cloves garlic, finely sliced
1 fresh long green chilli, finely sliced
2 cm piece ginger, grated finely
1 tsp chilli flakes
¼ tsp tumeric
400ml can coconut milk
375ml carton fish stock
1 T fish sauce
750gm firm white fish (snapper, sea perch,
tarakihi, ling, gurnard)
lemon juice

Method:
1. Sauté first 7 ingredients
2. Add stock, coconut milk & fish sauce
3. Add fish, cut into chunks, simmer 3-5 mins
or until fish is cooked through
4. Serve with rice and a squeeze of lemon juice

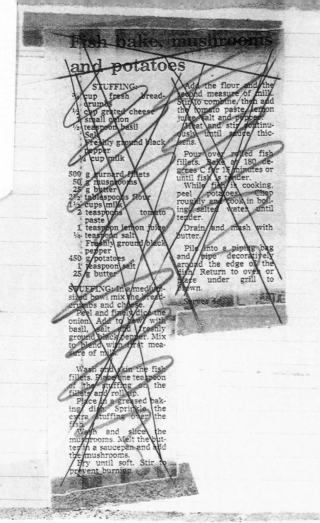

Fish bake, mushrooms and potatoes ~~(crossed out)~~

STUFFING:
¾ cup fresh bread-crumbs
¼ cup grated cheese
small onion
½ teaspoon basil
Salt
Freshly ground black pepper
¼ cup milk

500 g gurnard fillets
50 g mushrooms
25 g butter
2½ tablespoons flour
1½ cups milk
2 teaspoons tomato paste
1 teaspoon lemon juice
¼ teaspoon salt
Freshly ground black pepper
450 g potatoes
1 teaspoon salt
25 g butter

STUFFING: In a medium-sized bowl mix the bread-crumbs and cheese.
Peel and finely dice the onion. Add to bowl with basil, salt and freshly ground black pepper. Mix to blend with first measure of milk.

Wash and skin the fish fillets. Place one teaspoon of the stuffing on the fillets and roll up.
Place in a greased baking dish. Sprinkle the extra stuffing over the fish.
Wash and slice the mushrooms. Melt the butter in a saucepan and add the mushrooms.
Fry until soft. Stir to prevent burning.

Add the flour and the second measure of milk. Stir to combine, then add the tomato paste, lemon juice, salt and pepper.
Heat and stir continuously until sauce thickens.

Pour over rolled fish fillets. Bake at 180 degrees C for 15 minutes or until fish is tender.
While fish is cooking, peel potatoes. Chop roughly and cook in boiling salted water until tender.
Drain and mash with butter.

Pile onto a piping bag and pipe decoratively around the edge of the dish. Return to oven or place under grill to brown.

Serves 4

Batter for Fried Fish

1 cup flour
1 tsp salt
little white pepper
½ tsp Baking Soda } Sift

Mix in gradually —
1 tsp vinegar
2 tab. oil
About cup cold water.

Add a little more water if too stiff. Flour fish - dust off.
Use tongs to dip in batter.
Let stand awhile.

SMOKED FISH PIE

Ingredients: 1 smoked fish - Kawai or snapper (500gms of flesh)
Sauce: 500ml milk, 2 T Butter, 2 T flour, Salt & Pepper.
2 Hard boiled eggs - cut into quarters
2 cups mashed potato
2 Tblesps. capers
½ cup chopped curly-leafed parsley
2 sheets puff pastry
1 beaten egg for glazing.

Method:
- Pull fish away from bones & skin, place in bottom of deepish casserole dish - or pie dish.
- Make the white sauce by melting the butter, add the flour and cook a few mins, slowly add the milk (heating it first helps reduce the chance of lumpyness) stirring with a whisk all the while, season with plenty of S & P.
- Place hard boiled eggs, capers & chopped parsley in with fish
- Pour over sauce
- Spread over mashed potato
- Pastry on top, glaze with beaten egg. • 200°C for 30 mins.

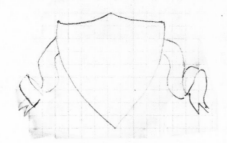

FANCY FISH PIE

(Serves 4)

This is a good alternative to smoked fish pie if
(i) you do not like smoked fish & (ii) your market does not sell smoked fish

① Poach some salmon fillets (enough for 2) and 2 small fillets of white fish e.g. (snapper, tarakihi, ling, seaperch,) in:
2 cups of milk, 2 onions - sliced, 3 bay leaves. 1 tsp peppercorns

② Carefully lift fish out with a slotted spoon and place in bottom of baking dish, strain off liquid for later use. Discard onion, Bay leaves

③ Meanwhile boil 3 medium sized potatoes for topping mash.

④ Make a white sauce with 2 T butter & 3 T flour, cooking this slightly first then adding the leftover poaching liquid to make a sauce. add salt & pepper

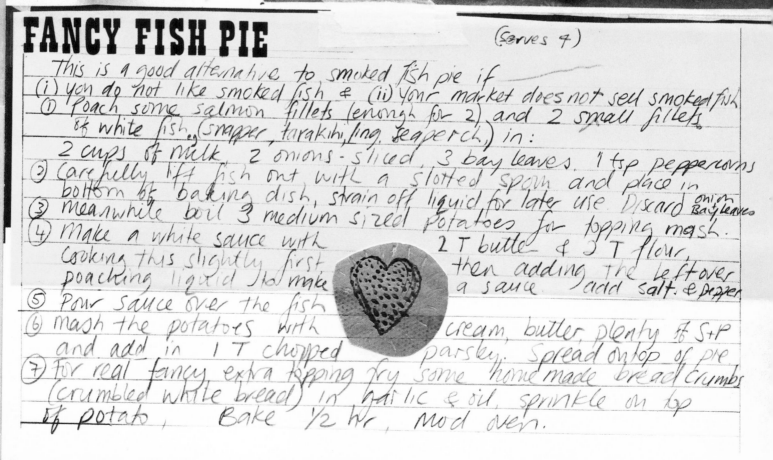

⑤ Pour sauce over the fish

⑥ mash the potatoes with cream, butter, plenty of S+P and add in 1 T chopped parsley. spread on top of pie

⑦ For real fancy extra topping fry some home made bread crumbs (crumbled white bread) in garlic & oil, sprinkle on top of potato. Bake ½ hr, mod oven.

Koala

Koala

Dingo

Kangaroo

Kangaroo

Australi

PRAWNS & BEER
ingredients:
1 1⁄4 kg cooked prawns
    (schoolies are best for this)
Beer
    (Coopers Pale Ale or
        Cascade Light)
Beach at sunset
Friends
Method:
Mix it up

Prawns
&
Beer

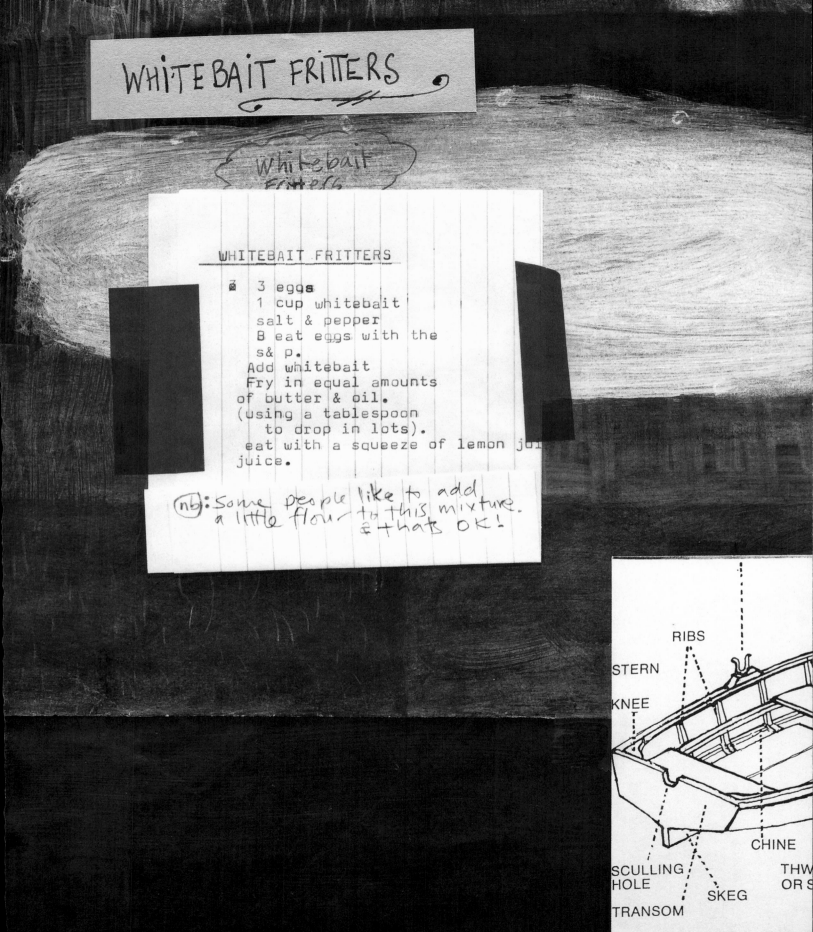

WHITEBAIT FRITTERS

Whitebait
Fritters

WHITEBAIT FRITTERS

```
ø  3 eggs
   1 cup whitebait
   salt & pepper
   B eat eggs with the
   s& p.
   Add whitebait
   Fry in equal amounts
 of butter & oil.
 (using a tablespoon
    to drop in lots).
   eat with a squeeze of lemon jui
 juice.
```

(nb): Some people like to add
a little flour to this mixture.
& thats OK!

RIBS

STERN

KNEE

CHINE

SCULLING
HOLE

THW
OR S

SKEG

TRANSOM

If you can swim, there is

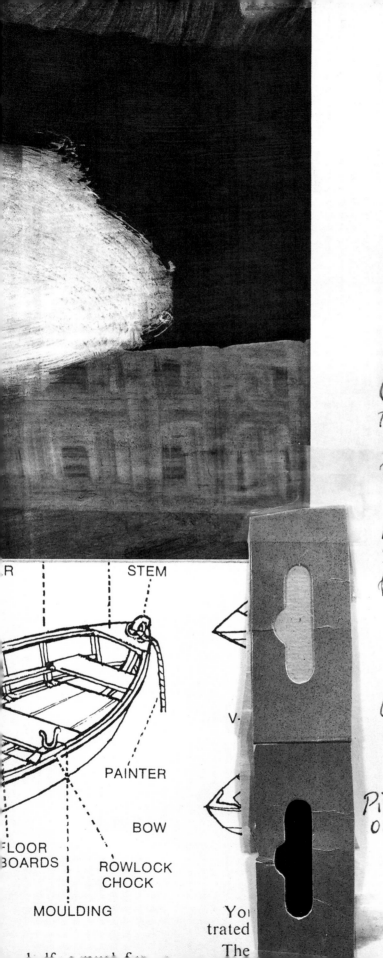

PiPi FRITTERS:

Gather the pipis at Low tide feeling for the shells with your felt (feet). Keep the pipis in a bucket of fresh water — they will spit out any sand.

Steam open the shells on a BBQ or in a wok with a little water. Scoop out pipi meat & add the following:

3 eggs — beaten
2 T Flour
plenty of Salt & Pepper
+ (2 cups pipi meat.)

Cook in hot oil & butter mix (1 T of each) Flip over after 1 min, eat hot in sandwich with mayo & watercress.

Pipis are also just fine on their own steamed open & dipped into some malt vinegar.

STEM
R

PAINTER

BOW

FLOOR
BOARDS

ROWLOCK
CHOCK

MOULDING

V.

Yo
trated
The

Words

Solipsism - view that self is all that
exists or can be known
paradigm - example pattern
esp. of inflexion of word
polemic - controversial, disputatious,
controversy

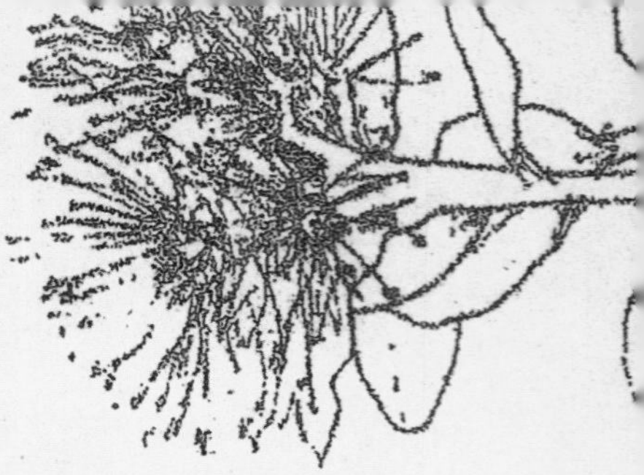

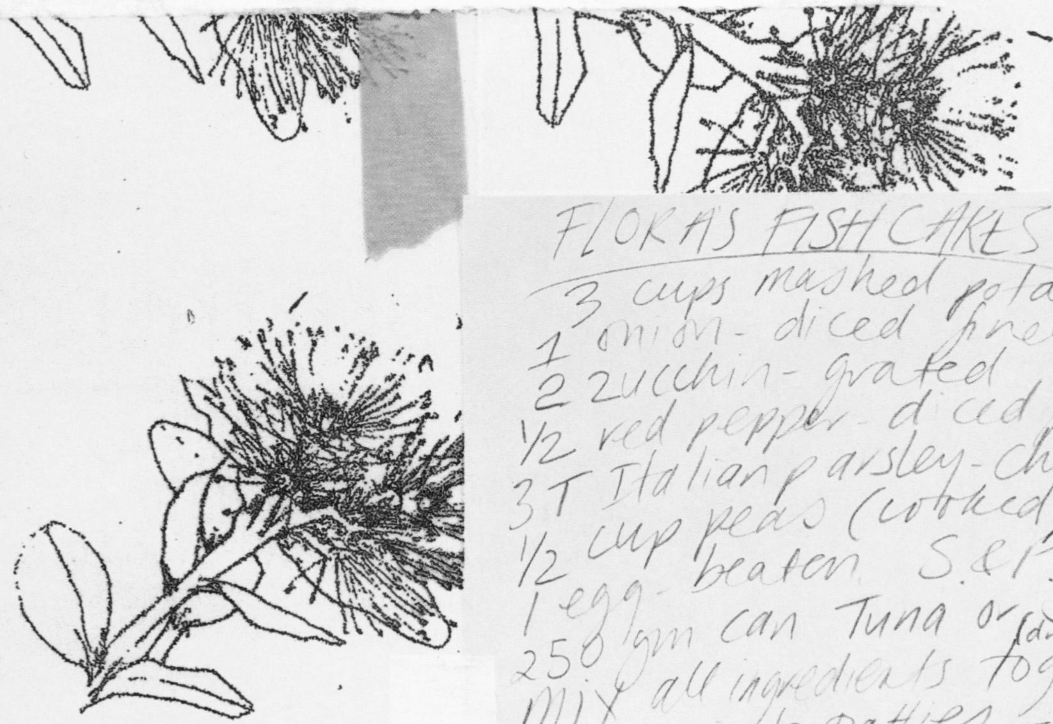

FLORA'S FISH CAKES
3 cups mashed potatoes
1 onion - diced finely
2 zucchini - grated
1/2 red pepper - diced finely
3 T Italian parsley - chopped
1/2 cup peas (cooked)
1 egg - beaten, S. & P.
250 gm can Tuna or Salmon (drained)
Mix all ingredients together
shape into patties - roll
in breadcrumbs & fry in
a mix of oil & butter.
Serve with lemon juice and
tartare sauce

Pohutu..

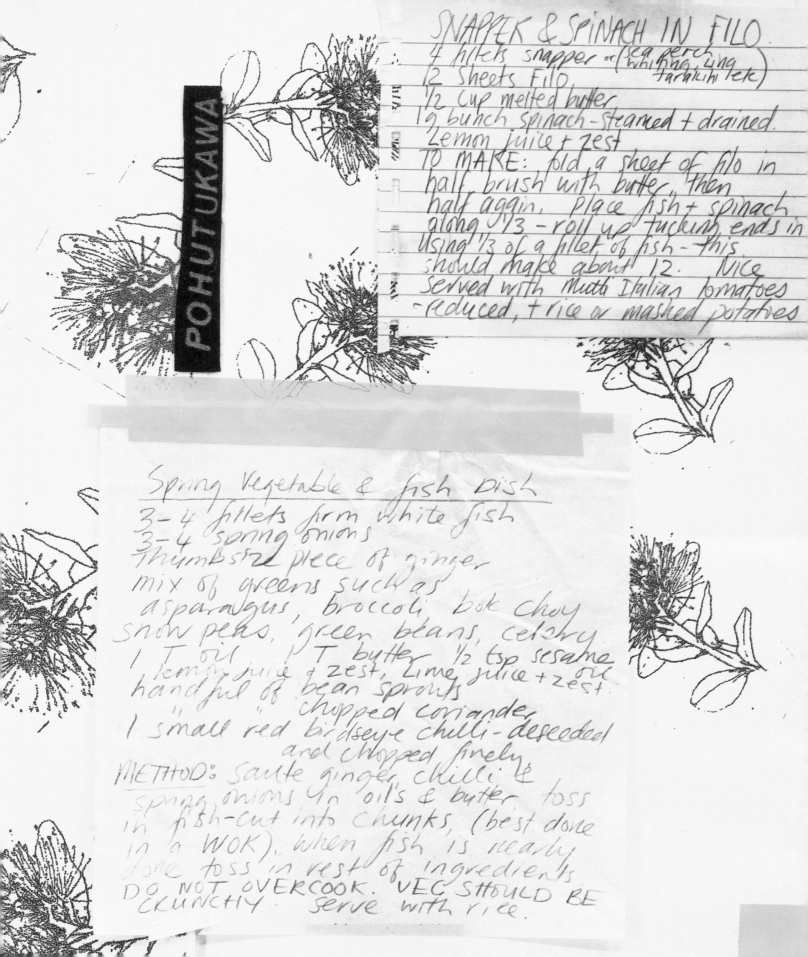

SNAPPER & SPINACH IN FILO

4 fillets snapper or (sea perch, whiting, ling, tarakihi etc)
12 sheets Filo
½ cup melted butter
1g bunch spinach - steamed + drained.
Lemon juice + zest

TO MAKE: fold a sheet of filo in half, brush with butter, then half again. Place fish + spinach along ⅓ - roll up tucking ends in using ⅓ of a fillet of fish - this should make about 12. Nice served with Mutti Italian tomatoes - reduced, + rice or mashed potatoes

POHUTUKAWA

Spring Vegetable & Fish Dish

3-4 fillets from white fish
3-4 spring onions
thumbsize piece of ginger
mix of greens such as
  asparagus, broccoli, bok choy
snow peas, green beans, celery.
1 T oil, 1 T butter ½ tsp sesame
lemon juice & zest, Lime juice + zest. oil
handful of bean sprouts
  " " chopped coriander
1 small red birdseye chilli - deseeded
        and chopped finely.
METHOD: saute ginger, chilli &
spring onions in oil's & butter toss
in fish - cut into chunks, (best done
in a WOK). When fish is nearly
done toss in rest of ingredients
DO NOT OVERCOOK. VEG SHOULD BE
CRUNCHY. serve with rice.

NOT FOR PUSS

Fishermans stew

spring onions
sauteed in butter,
dry white wine,
tarragon...add
creme fraiche
fish stock
salmon
snapper
scallops
puff pastry
make sauce
pour over chopped
fish - leave scallops
whole, pastry on top

bake 15 mins

when cutting fish
a sharp knife is
really important.
Everytime Mum
comes to stay she
buys me a new
knife sharpener

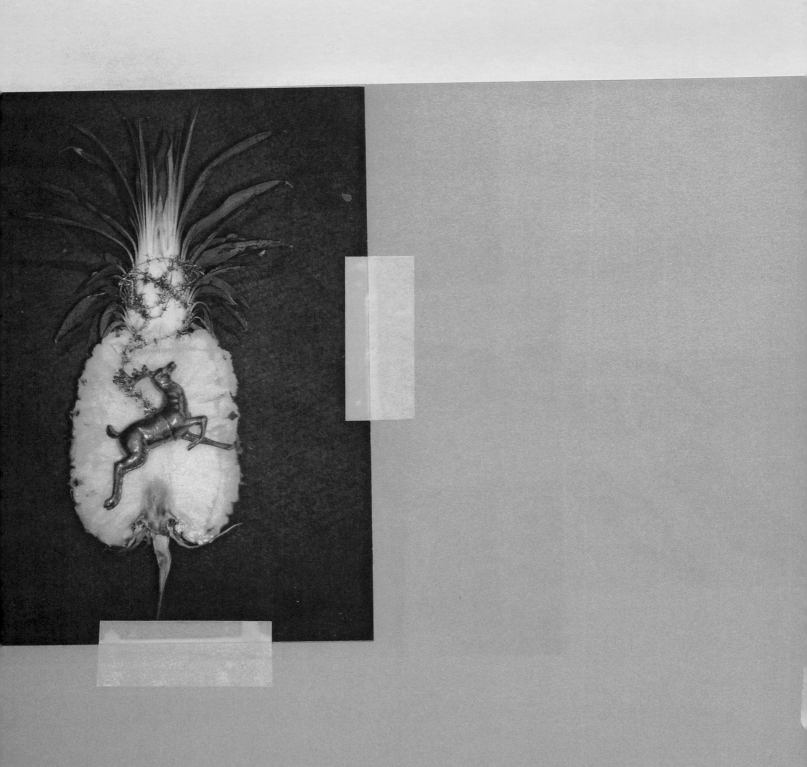

Curried Fish

mMum made this dish heaps of times throug
through out the 70's, at all her dinner
parties. We thought it very exotic.
I asked her to make it a while ago
& she refused. So I had a go and
it was fantastic. I used fresh pineapple
Mum used to use the canned stuff, which

was fine. She also used tomato sauce insteqd
of tomato relish, or maybe she had just run
out.
-***
4 Medium size fillets white fish, boaned &
    skinned, snapper(nz)..sea perch(Aust)
2 Tblesp butter
1 cup cream
2 teasp good curry powder
xax xxxxx sea salt, whit pepper
4 Thinly sliced rings of fresh pineapple
1 Tblesp chopped parsley
4 heaped tsp tomato relish

METHOD
Melt butter (just 1 tblesp)
fry fillets quickly, take out of pan,
add rest of butter and curry powder, cook
slowly add cream, stirring with wooden spoon
                                    spoon
Slip fish back into pan to reheat and compl
    complete cooking.
TO SERVE :
Place a fillet on each plate, spoon over sauce
Place ring of pineapple on top of each fillet
and a dab of relish on one side of pineapple
and sprinkle of parsley on other side, spoon
rest of sauce from pan alonside fish.
Great with steamed rice.

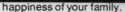
happiness of your family.

Baked Snapper on Beds of Tofu

(Serves four)

I invented this recipe after having something similar
for Yum Cha in Sydney's China Town. This dish is really easy
to assemble and is meltingly delicious.
The combination of rice, fish, tofu and greens works really
well particularly with the different textures.
Also, needless to say this is a very healthy dinner!

4 small fish fillets, (or larger fillets, cut in half)
 You can use any of your favourite types of fish:
tarakihi, sea perch, whiting, gurnard,
although I think a more solid firmer fish is best.
2 blocks firm tofu
2T sunflower oil
½ cup tamari or good soy sauce
4 spring onions, cut into 4-5 cm lengths
handful chopped coriander
handful ripped basil leaves
handful cherry tomatoes, halved
1T sesame seeds
zest and juice of 1 lime and 1 lemon
salt & pepper

Slice tofu into 4 'beds' by cutting the blocks into half
through the middle, so that each piece will act as bed to lay
the fish on.
Grease your baking dish with 1T of the oil, arrange the 4
beds in the dish so they are touching but not overlapping.
Sprinkle the beds with ½ the tamari, ½ the zest & juice of the
lemon & lime, S&P
Lay the fish on the beds, sprinkle over rest of ingredients,
except for the fresh coriander and basil
Bake 30 mins, mod oven.
Remove from oven, plate up with the coriander, basil and an
extra squeeze of lemon juice, best served with steaming hot
jasmine or basmati rice.
Nb. If you want this dish to be spicy add chilli paste or a
deseeded thinly sliced birdseye red chilli

AUSTRALIA

AUSTRALIA

AUSTRALIA
COMMONWEALTH

3

Crumbed fish with Hot Potato Salad

This dish was a regular at our family table, and a favorite with everyone.
We always used skinned and boned snapper, but other fish such as gurnard, whiting, sea perch, actually any white, firm-fleshed fish works in this simple dish.

Crumbed Fish:

1-2 eggs, beaten
1 reasonable sized fillet of fish per person, cut in half, on the diagonal
1-2 cups white breadcrumbs, (packaged are best)
2 Tblesp flour
salt & pepper
2 Tblesp vegetable oil
2 Tblesp butter

Rinse and pat dry the fillets of fish with paper towel, this is to remove any leftover scales, take off any skin that may remain and feel carefully for any forgotten bones, pulling them away to discard.
Season the flour with plenty of salt and pepper.
Dredge the fillets through the flour then dip into the beaten egg and lastly coat with the breadcrumbs.
Fry fish in large frypan, in a mix of the butter & oil on medium heat turning once.
Fish should be golden brown on both sides.
Serve with wedges of lemon & tartare sauce

Hot Potato Salad:

4-5 medium sized potatoes, peeled and sliced quite thinly
2 Tblesp olive oil
1 red pepper – deseeded and sliced thinly
2 medium sized onions – sliced thinly into rings
2 cups hot water, or vegetable stock
4 hardboiled eggs roughly chopped,
salt & pepper
2 Tblesp chopped parsley

Put the oil into a wide saucepan, when nearly smoking toss in the potatoes, cook for a few mins, stirring constantly, add the onion, cook for a few more minutes then add the red pepper. Season with salt & pepper, add the stock or water, put the lid on the pot, turn the heat down and simmer for 20 mins, stirring occasionally.
Turn out onto a serving dish, garnish with the chopped egg & parsley.

Quick Tartare Sauce

Mix together equal amounts of mayonnaise, & sour cream, add a handful of chopped capers and 3 small gherkins, finely diced, finish with a squeeze of lemon juice, s& p.

I did catch this fish (and broke the rod). It was such a shock to land this enormous and very old snapper. This is the first fish I ever caught — and my LAST — I'm done! John G smoked this for me. & we spread it around the neighbourhood.

Tuna & Spinach Bake

500g spinach steamed & pureed
250g bacon sliced & crisped
Combine above with $\frac{1}{2}$ cup
breadcrumbs, 1 cup sour cream
salt & pepper, juice of 1 lemon,
2 cans 220g tuna in spring water,
(drained) and lastly 2 T fresh
parmesan, finely grated.
Stir well,
top with more parmesan
Bake mod oven,(350 degrees C)
20 mins.
Good with rice and green salad.

chicken

Chicken Stewed With Red Wine

500gms chicken breast
500gms chicken thighs
½ cup of flour
small handful of thyme leaves
2 T oil
1 large onion diced finely
3 cloves garlic sliced very finely
2 cups sliced mushrooms
4 rashers bacon, rind removed and sliced finely
2 carrots peeled and sliced
2 sticks celery finely sliced
2 potatoes peeled and diced
1 cup red wine
3 bay leaves
3 T tomato paste
2 cans Italian tomatoes, Mutti brand give the best flavour for this
1 cup vegetable or chicken stock
salt & pepper

Saute the garlic & onion with the bacon until onion is transparent. Transfer to a casserole dish.
Saute the celery, carrot, mushrooms and thyme in the oil, for a few minutes, add in to the garlic & onion mix.
Dredge the chicken (cut up into chunky pieces) through the flour and fry in same pan adding a little more oil if needed, when browned, add to casserole dish, sprinkle over the thyme leaves, tuck in the bay leaves, pour over tomatoes, & wine. At this moment you can add in the diced potatoes.
Deglaze frypan with the stock, reserving a little of the liquid to mix in the tomato paste. Pour all this into the casserole dish, season with plenty of salt & pepper, cover and bake slowly moderate - low oven, for one hour.
Garnish with heaps of chopped Italian flat leaved parsley.

Tastes even better the next day.

ITALIAN CHICKEN

8 chicken pieces
2T flour
1/4 cup oil 60g butter
6 shallots, chopped
2 chicken stock cubes
1/2 cup white wine
1 cup sliced mushrooms
1/2 cup chopped Italian parsley

METHOD: Coat chicken in flour & fry in
oil & butter, remove with slotted
spoon when lightly browned.
Place in casserole dish with
remaining ingredients, except parsley.
Cover & cook 40 mins 180°C
garnish with parsley

Chicken Garden-Isley
Chicken Breasts
Sliced 3/4 way through
Stuff with ham & mozzerella mozzerella
  (or swiss
  cheese)
-Coat in egg & breadcrumbs
Bake Mod oven 40 mins,
turning once.

(had to
google
that!)

?

OTHER STUFFINGS:

(i) spinach, mushrooms & ricotta
(ii) green mango, coconut, ginger & feta
(iii) mustard, (seeded) gruyère cheese
    and asparagus!

chick breast
cream cheese for spread
  sundried tom
Spinach leaves
onion + tom
simmer.   sauce.
serve basil and
parmesan

Bede
26/07/04

CAULIFLOWER, CHICKEN & CAPERBERRY CASSEROLE

"2 cans ~~crushed~~ crushed tomatoes
1 large breast chicken - cut into smallish chunks & browned
                          quickly in olive oil
2 small zucchinis - ~~sliced on the diagonal~~
½ red capsicum - sliced
2 T tomato paste
2 T caperberries - found in your supermarket next to the olives
2 cups cooked (al dente) farfelle, (bow shaped) pasta
2 T crumbled feta
½ cauliflower broken up & steamed

Method:

Layer all of the above in a large, shallow casserole dish
in any order - although the feta is best on the top.
Bake uncovered for 30 mins, moderate oven.

Additional (optional) topping

While the casserole is cooking,
slice an eggplant into half, lengthwise,
then into ½ moon shapes, about 1cm wide.
sprinkle liberally with sea salt.
Leave for 10 mins then wipe off liquid that forms
(these are the bitter juices)
Place eggplant slices onto a greased oven tray, sprinkle
with plenty of olive oil and cover with breadcrumbs.
Bake in the same oven as the chicken, plce on the rack
above the casserole. Eggplant should be ~~golden~~ golden brown after
15 mins. Serve on top of ~~chicken~~ dish.
                              chicken

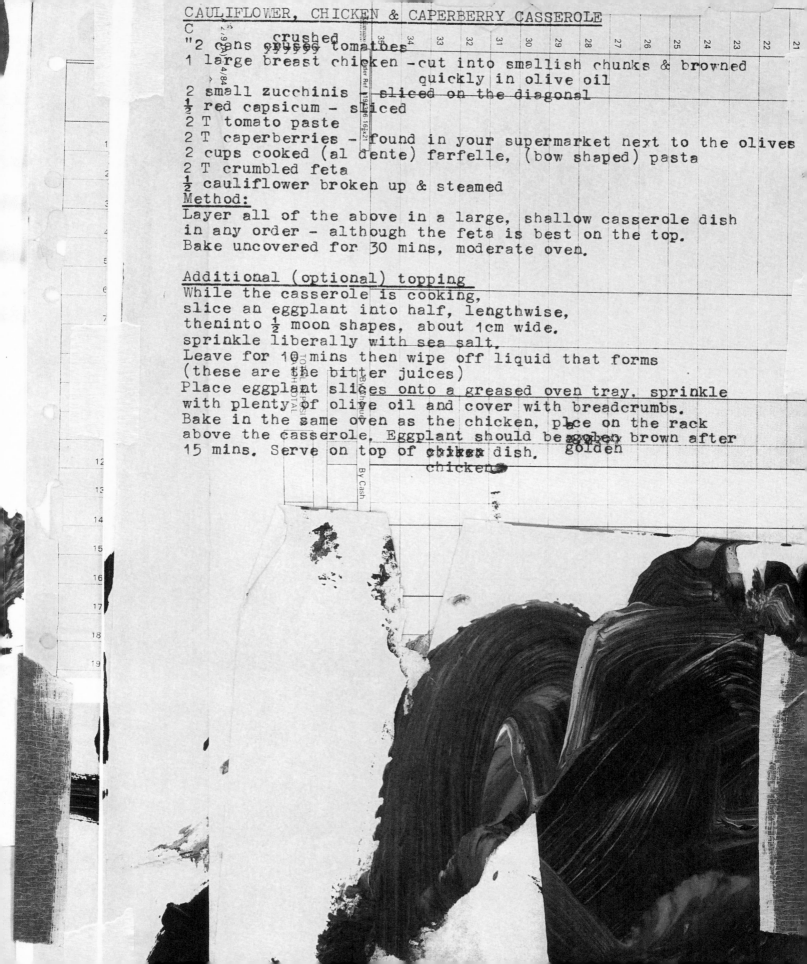

Cast off at beg of next and every row 5[5:6:6]sts twice, 5sts twice, 4sts twice and 2sts 6 times.

Complete as given for Back from ** to **.

Neckband

Join left shoulder seam. Using No. 10 needles and B and with RS facing, K up 144[148:152:156]sts evenly round neck.

1st row *K1 tbl, P1, rep from * to end.

Rep 1st row 7 times more.

Next row *K1 tbl, yfwd, sl 1, ybk, rep from * to end.

Rep last row 3 times more. Cast off by invisible method as given for Skirt. Join right shoulder seam and neckband.

Armbands

Using No.10 needles and B and with RS facing, K up 129[133:137:141]sts evenly around armhole.

from * to end.

2nd row K1 tbl, P2 tog, rib to last 3sts, P2 tog, K1 tbl.

Rep 1st and 2nd rows 3 times more.

Complete as for Neckband.

To make up

Press all pieces under a damp cloth with a warm iron.

Skirt. Join side seams. Thread elastic through casing st at waist, joining ends to form a circle. Press seams. Using No.3·00 (ISR) hook and B, join yarn at side seam and work 1 round dc around bottom edge. Join with a ss. Work 2 rounds crab st, twisting sts by working in dc from left to right instead of right to left. Fasten off.

Bolero top. Join side seams and Armbands.

Remove casting on thread, see Knitting Know-how, chapter 2. Thread elastic through casing st at lower edge, joining ends to form a circle.

▲ *Sleeveless bolero top and abbreviated skirt for cool-day sun bathing*

▼ *Contrasting diamond motifs link the white bolero to the navy skirt*

Smoked Chicken & Leek Pie

1 smoked chicken - (these should be readily available from your
                local supermarket)
2 T olive oil
2 T butter
2 medium sized leeks - trimmed and sliced into rings, (use
                about 1/3 of the green stems as well as the white)
2 medium sized carrots — peeled, halved lengthways and sliced
                thinly on the diagonal
2 sticks celery — sliced thinly on the diagonal
small handful fresh Thyme
2 T plain white flour
1/2 cup white wine
2 cups full cream milk
ground black pepper
2 sheets puff pastry
1 egg — beaten

Method:

Sauté leeks, carrots & celery in the butter and oil, seasoning
with pepper - no salt as smoked chicken is usually already quite
salty. Add diced chicken meat.
Sprinkle flour over this mixture and cook for a further 2 mins.
Slowly add white wine, then the milk, simmer along slowly and
reduce liquid a little, the sauce should thicken nicely.
Pour mixture into a pie dish, cover with the pastry, don't
forget to make some leaf decorations ……… brush with the beaten
egg and into moderate oven 20 mins or until the pastry is

Chicken Curry

This recipe provides a great base for experimenting with, adding
 more spices, or substituting ingredients, depending on your preferences.

Ingredients:
3 T butter
3 T vegetable oil
3 cloves garlic, thinly sliced
thumbsized piece of fresh ginger, grated, skin and all
1 onion, finely diced
2 tsp tumeric
2 tsp coriander
1 tsp cumin
1 tsp garam masala
1 tsp coriandar seeds
1tsp cumin seeds
2 birdseye chillis, finely sliced, deseeded if you want a milder curry
1 cup natural yogurt
1 can crushed tomatoes
1 can water
1 kg chicken meat, diced, (no skin or bones)
juice of 1 lemon, heaps fresh chopped coriander
salt and pepper

Method:
Melt together butter & oil in a heavy bottomed saucepan, add garlic,
onion and ginger first, sauté for a few mins until the onion is transparent,
add all the other spices, sweating them off for a few minutes, add the can
of tomatoes, juice and all and the other can of water.
Simmer for bit longer, add in the chicken, turn down the heat and simmer
Slowly. Season with plenty of salt and pepper, when the chicken is cooked,
after about 40 mins stir in the yogurt. Serve with steamed rice, sqeeze of
lemon juice and the chopped fresh coriander.

Variations:
Add in long green beans, diced potatoes, fresh spinach leaves, fresh tomatoes
Serve with cucumber raita and chapatis.

Pizza base
Dissolved it
Milk
Wipes.
Bowl.
Spoon
Plate
dishwash liquid.
gloves.
Light for Laptop.
Soda Stim liquid
Sugar   Bun

3 Red onions.
Garlic.
Carrots
+ Field mushrooms.
Eg. Brisket or Stewing
        Beef.
Dog. Puff Pastry All Butter.
loaves.
nappy wipes.
milk - fruit.

light bulbs.
Milk
eggs
breadcrumbs
apples
Fish
(me) 251.

Fish
corn chips
Pastry -
Pizza shapes
BBQ crackers
rice
pasta
doughnuts

Butter
Bread
Milk
ICE CREAM
Beans

milk
onions
tuna
meat x1
bread x2
oranges & fruit.
mexican - R beans, burritos
canned toms
tomatoes.
cereal.
toilet paper . . . . .

Camera batt
insect repell

2 #20 chicken
1 #16
1 #18 chick
1 Roasting Fowl
2 bag cassava.
6 ctn CBBS.
2 x g - fish fillet

Stardust
Film fair.

Milk (Mum's + Dv
Beard
Biscuits.
Rice Bubbles
Corn Flakes
Soft Drinks
Steam Pudding
Fish oil Tabets
Palmolive
Rubbish Bags
Handle Towels
ice cream.
Seeto Pack
Pet food

hummous
crackers
lime juice
Soda H2O
sauce
Chick
condensed milk
van ice cream
wafers
cherries
slivered almonds
bread
milk
mayo

List 1 (bold marker):
Mince
Cheese
Toms
Pasta
prods
Sour cream

List 2 (top):
Bacon
Red Onion
Lettuce
Cucumber
Milk
Pumkin

List 3:
SARDINES
BALLS
TOOTHPASTE
RAZORS
MARMITE

List 4:
Onions
Milk
Strawberri
Cauli
Coffee
Sugar
PK

List 5 (top):
dishwasher
Olive oil
eggs
corn chips
Bisc
Icing sugar
cheerios
Saus. rolls
100 & 1000's
Orange juice
potato chips
Ham
can asp.
(mini crunchie
Lollie Pops
Canned cream
pass the parcel

List 6:
tent
sleeping mats
cups
knives / forks / spoons
plates
cutting board
cooking
esky

List 7 (right):
Potatoes
Waldorf
chargrilled
marinated
chicken
Lamb
green salad

Feta
Carrots
Walnuts
rocket
french
cucumber
avo
Milk
Ice cream
Pop chips
ground almond
Meat

List 8:
Soap powder
Rubbish Bag
Paper towel
Dettol Soap

Carrots
Lettuce
Onions

List 9 (bottom left):
chicken / leek pie
chick breast + thighs
Leeks x 2
mushrooms
chicken stock
celery
cream
Beetroot salad
Bacon, Cherry Toms
Beetroots
feta
rocket
salad
cous cous
rosemary

List 10:
Banana splits
Bananas
Vanilla Ice cream
wafers
6 adults
4 kids
Thurs:
Beetroots
chick pie filling
green sauce

List 11 (bottom middle):
Bread
Jam
Milk
Vegemite
Melo
Bananas
fruit bisc.
Herbal T.

French onion chicken with apricots

Serves 4

1kg skinless chicken pieces, trimmed
(see note)

1 onion, sliced

45g packet French onion soup (or
chicken noodle)

840g can apricots in natural juice

125g green beans, trimmed

1 Place chicken pieces into a large casserole dish (see variation). Sprinkle evenly with onion rings and soup.

2 Stir apricots and juice into dish. Bake, covered, in a moderate oven (180°C) for 1 hour or until chicken is tender.

3 Stir beans through casserole. Serve immediately with noodles or potatoes.

Variation If preferred, dust chicken pieces in flour and brown in a frying pan sprayed with cooking oil before arranging in the casserole dish.

---

sliced.

Method:

Melt the butter in a saucepan. Add the tomatoes, garlic, tabasco and worcestershire sauces. Season with salt and pepper.

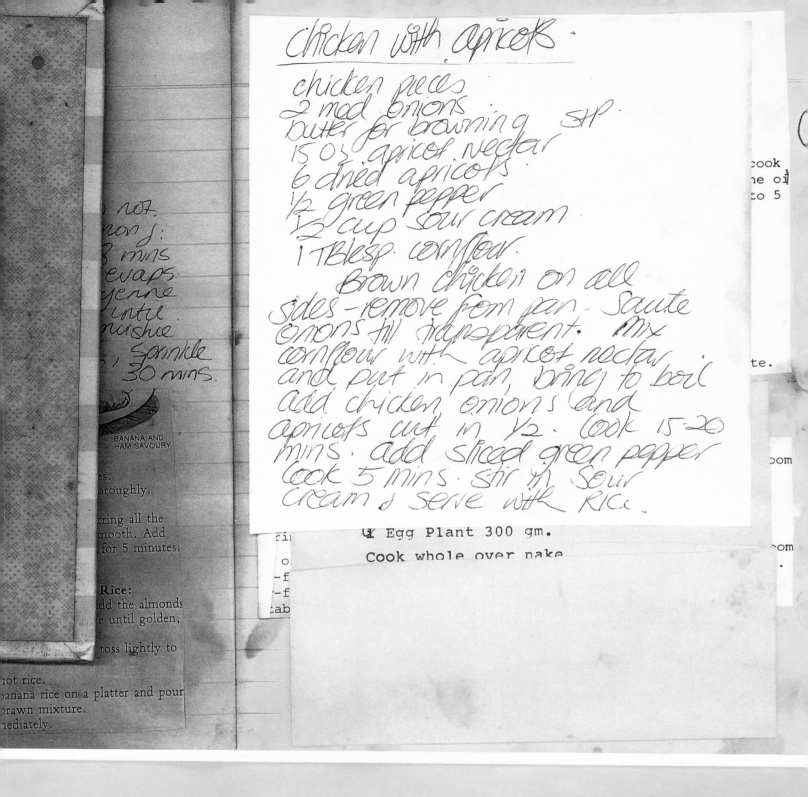

Chicken with apricots

chicken pieces
2 med onions
butter for browning S/P
15 oz apricot nectar
6 dried apricots
1/2 green pepper
1/2 cup sour cream
1 TBlesp. cornflour.

Brown chicken on all sides - remove from pan. Saute onions till transparent. Mix cornflour with apricot nectar and put in pan, bring to boil add chicken, onions and apricots cut in 1/2. Cook 15-20 mins. add sliced green pepper cook 5 mins. Stir in sour cream & serve with rice.

4 Egg Plant 300 gm.
Cook whole over nake

BANANA AND
HAM SAVOURY

...es.
...oroughly.

...rring all the
...mooth. Add
...for 5 minutes.

...Rice:
...dd the almonds
...e until golden,

...toss lightly to

...ot rice.
...banana rice on a platter and pour
...prawn mixture.
...nediately.

...not.
...non j.
...8 mins
...evaps.
...yenne
...until.
...mushie
..., sprinkle
...30 mins.

Chicken Breast in Coconut Milk & Mango

Ingredients: (for four people)
4 pieces of boned chicken breast
1-2 limes, (depending on size)
1 greenish mango (not too ripe)
100ml thick coconut milk or coconut cream
1T sunflower oil
2 spring onions
1 pinch ground ginger and/or cayenne pepper
Salt & pepper

Method:
1. Cut each piece of breast in ½ lengthwise &
   season with plenty of s&p, juice & zest of lime,
   ginger/cayenne pepper
2. Peel and slice mango, reserving juice
3. Mix 1 T of coconut cream, & sunflower oil into frypan,
   snip in spring onions, sauté for 1-2 mins, stirring all
   the while, add chicken and cook for about 2 mins on each side.
4. Add remaining coconut cream, mango slices and any mango
   juice. Cover pan and simmer gently for about 8 mins,
   turning chicken over halfway through.
5. Transfer chicken and mango to warmed plates, boil sauce
   to reduce, adjust seasoning, pour reduced sauce over
   chicken & mango, serve with rice & something green.

Variation:
Leaving out the ginger and cayenne pepper, crush in some
green peppercorns just before reducing sauce.

The recipe:

Chicken Florentine.

Fry halved Tomatoes in garlic and olive oil, make enough to cover the bottom of the deep baking dish you are using. If the tomatoes are big you make want to slice them into 4 thick slices. I slice off the top and bottom pieces. Once the tomatos are turning slightly golden, flip over cook 2nd side then transfer to baking dish.

Cover the tomatoes with either a large bunch of steamed fresh spinach chopped, or a package of frozen spinach, defrosted and juice sqeezed out, in all about 2 cups.

Sprinkle plenty of salt and pepper over spinach.

Using either a cooked chicken or chicken breast sliced and cooked, either steamed or sauteed, doesn't really matter, just needs to be cooked. Dice the chicken and place on top of spinach. You will realise you need to assemble this pie in a deep wide dish.

Make a white sauce by melting 3 Tblespoons butter, adding 2 tblesp. Flour, cooking this a little until beginning to brown, then slowly add a cup of milk, then a cup of ceam , S & P.

Add another cup of milk or until the sauce is of a good consistency, pour over chicken, spinach and tomato mixture.

Top pie with bread crumbs or small cubes turkish bread or any left over bread,

finally add a layer of grated parmesan, plenty more S & P.

Cook about 30-40 mins in mod oven until crust is golden brown,

serves about 6 - 10, depending on size of dish you are using.

PAINTINGS + DRAWINGS

Date

BEE ALERT | BEEHIVE SAFETY SUGGESTIONS

107X71mm

lady's Smock Shepherd's purse
me not speedwell
Speedwell Speedwell
speedwell

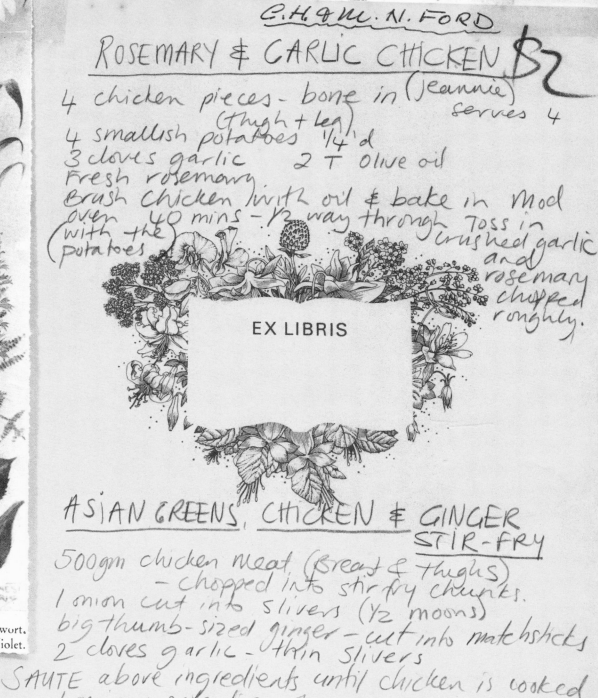

C.H. & M.N. FORD

ROSEMARY & GARLIC CHICKEN $2

(Jeannie)
serves 4

4 chicken pieces - bone in (thigh + leg)
4 smallish potatoes 1/4'd
3 cloves garlic   2 T Olive oil
Fresh rosemary

Brush Chicken with oil & bake in Mod oven 40 mins - 1/2 way through Toss in (with the potatoes) crushed garlic and rosemary chopped roughly.

ASIAN GREENS, CHICKEN & GINGER STIR-FRY

500gm chicken meat (Breast & thighs)
 - chopped into stir fry chunks.
1 onion cut into slivers (1/2 moons)
big thumb-sized ginger - cut into matchsticks
2 cloves garlic - thin slivers

SAUTE above ingredients until chicken is cooked
toss in a selection of:
  bok choy, broccolini, chinese spinach
  baby spinach leaves, (go to markets to get greens - experiment with the unfamiliar)

QUICKLY add in Lime juice
  chilli sauce for chicken. S & P
  large handful of bean sprouts
SERVE with rice & soy sauce + coriander

py.   4—Goat's Beard.   5—Stitchwort.
-Coltsfoot.   10—Primrose.   11—Violet.

meats

...iant floor cushion

...lightweight, comfortable floor
...on is big enough to seat an
... The foam stuffing is contained
... undercover which unzips for
... filling if needed; the outer cover
...s for washing. For firmness, the
...is made from two thicknesses of
... plus a layer of heavy-duty
...acing.

...oose a sturdy fabric for the outer
..., and make sure that it is wash-
... The undercover can be made
... calico, muslin, or any similar
...weight, inexpensive fabric.

...erials needed
... of 115 cm fabric for outer cover
... of 115 cm fabric for under-
...ver
... of 90 cm heavy-duty iron-on
...erfacing
... 45 cm zippers
... of 12 mm cotton tape
... of shredded foam
...opriate thread

...ng
...rcover Cut two rectangles
... the lengthwise grain, each
...uring 48 × 142 cm. Cut one
... with a 92 cm diameter, and two
...ircles, each with a 92 cm diam-
...and an added 1 cm seam allow-
...on the straight edge.

...r cover Cut two 63 cm ×
...m rectangles across the width of
...abric, and one 63 × 70 cm rec-
...e across the width of the fabric
...e will be pieced to form one long
...ngle). For the base, cut four
...ircles, each with a 94 cm diam-
...and an added 1 cm allowance on
...traight edge.

...t two semicircles from the iron-
... interfacing, each 90 cm in
...eter.

...r the button, cut two circles with
... diameters from the cover

fabric and two with 14 cm diameters
from the iron-on interfacing.

Assembly
Undercover Staystitch the long
edges of both rectangles. With right
sides facing, pin and machine-stitch
the ends of the two large rectangles
together. Press seam open. Pin and
stitch other ends together to form a
circular body.

With right sides facing, pin the
circle to one end of the undercover;
clip the seam allowances of the undercover as necessary to go around the
curves. Machine-stitch as pinned.

Pin the straight edges of the two

semicircles together and machine-
stitch at each end, leaving a 45 cm
opening in the centre. Insert zipper in
opening. Attach zippered circle to
undercover same way as first circle.

Turn the unde...
side and fill it ...
foam. Close zippe...
Outer cover St...
edge of all thre...
right sides facing,...
stitch edges of re...
form one circular...
that fabric patter...
same direction...
seams open.

Place two r...

stitches between each sea...
ing along the unstaystit...
one a thread's width a...
allowance line, the ot...
higher. Leave long thread...

Irish Stew (mum)

1 Kg of lamb chops.   I like to use loin as they are
tender but chump ones are cheaper.

Cut as much fat off as possible, they can be left whole
or cut into pieces, salt and pepper and then brown in
a little butter and oil.

Remove meat, brown two finely sliced onions.   Add cup
 and a half of water to the pan, scraping off all the
brown bits.

Place all in a casserole dish, add one finely cut up carrot
and parsnip and cook slowly for one and a half to two hours.
Remove dish and add a tin of drained peas or frozen ones.
Tbls of mint sauce is a nice option to add at this stage.

Mix 1 tbs of flour into half a tbls of butter,
blend well and then add to mixture to thicken,
pop back into over for half an hour.
If any of the flour and butter
is floating on the top, gently mash it against the
side.

Serve with mashed potatoes.

(Tracey & Jo)

Curried Sausages.

1 kilo pork sausages.

Boil to remove fat.

(Two thirds)

3 big | 2/3 carrots ⟶ Grated ⟶ **6** med
1 big | 1/3 parsnips ⟶ 2 med.

- Melt 2 tblspoons butter in large saucepan.
- Add Clive of India curry powder 3 heaped teaspoons. Cook for 2 mins

Add grated carrot + parsnip
+ chicken stock — 5 ~~2 3~~ cups
+ ~~one 1 cup~~ 1 3/4 ~~1½ cups~~ sultanas
Cook for few minutes +
add cut up sausages.

Simmer for 20-40 mins.

Thicken with ~~either~~ cornflour
~~of flour + butter~~ . mixed into paste with water

Makes heaps!!
Freezes well!

Specially painted for this work by Ellis Silas.

A CLIPPER ON THE HOMEWARD RUN

...mous as well as most graceful of all sailing-ships were the Clippers, a special type of ...wed vessel built for quick sailing and chiefly employed in the China tea trade. The days ...great races to be first home with the season's new tea were between 1850 and 1870, and ...rd for the run between Hong Kong and London was just under 80 days. With the opening of the Suez Canal the era of the Clippers passed away.

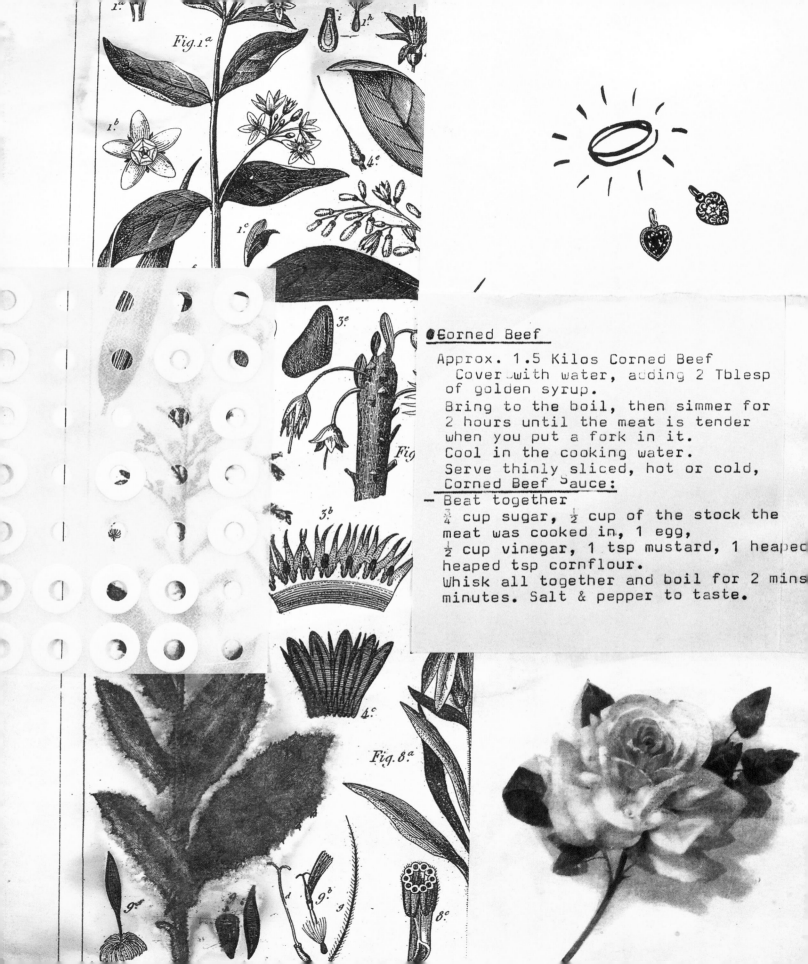

Corned Beef

Approx. 1.5 Kilos Corned Beef
  Cover with water, adding 2 Tblesp
of golden syrup.
Bring to the boil, then simmer for
2 hours until the meat is tender
when you put a fork in it.
Cool in the cooking water.
Serve thinly sliced, hot or cold,
Corned Beef Sauce:
- Beat together
$\frac{3}{4}$ cup sugar, $\frac{1}{2}$ cup of the stock the
meat was cooked in, 1 egg,
$\frac{1}{2}$ cup vinegar, 1 tsp mustard, 1 heaped
heaped tsp cornflour.
Whisk all together and boil for 2 mins
minutes. Salt & pepper to taste.

"FIRST SNOW". Mount Ngauruhoe. By Leonard Long.
One of three major volcanic mountains of Tongariro National Park, symmetrical
and dramatic in appearance it rises to 7,515 feet.

ISLAND

LLono

Beef Stir Fry:

(serves 4)

3 medium sized sirloin steaks
2 cloves garlic - sliced finely (+ peeled)
1 small red birdseye chilli, deseeded
                    & sliced very finely.

3 T soysauce or tamari
2 T vegetable cooking oil
1 large handful of long green beans
1 cup sliced mushrooms - blanched.
½ cup boiling water.

Marinade the steak in the garlic,
chilli & soysauce (or tamari) for at
least 20 mins. Heat oil in wok
until nearly smoking, toss in meat &
marinade, cook; stirring for about
3 mins until most of the meat is
browned, then add the mushrooms
& the boiling water. Place lid over
the stir-fry, allowing the steam to
cook the mushrooms cook another
2 mins, uncover & add green beans,
toss & serve piping hot with juices.
* Goes best with fluffy white rice.

Basic Beef and Mushroom family casserole:

2 Tbsp olive oil
2 Tbsp plain flour
800g diced beef
1 lg onion, finely chopped
1 carrot, diced
1 stick celery, thinly sliced
2 cups sliced mushrooms
2 cloves garlic
1 carton vege stock (500mls)
splash red wine (½ cup)
chopped parsley for serving.

Method:

Heat oil, saute garlic (crushed) coat beef with flour - brown → toss into casserole dish, brown onions add to dish, deglaze with red wine, pour into dish. add vegetables, mushrooms and stock. add salt + pepper to taste. cover with tinfoil. baked in mod - low oven 1 hour. serve with rice or mashed potatoes. sprinkle parsley over the top.

You could add: peas frozen vegetables as spinach place of carrot + mushrooms

Mum
Dad
Lee
Tracey
Fran
Joe
(& bunny)

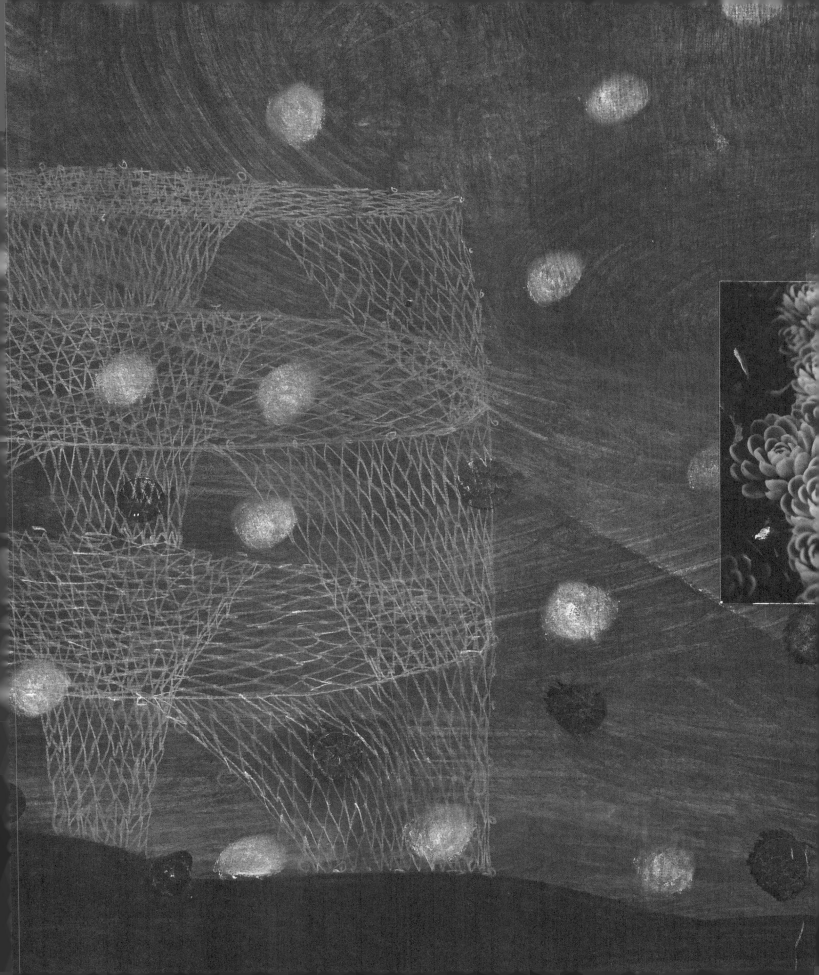

Beef Wellington

This dish was considered very fancy in
the 60,s & 70,s. Suitable to present for a dinner
party. Mum used to serve this with mashed potatoes
& green beans.

1 T olive oil
4 T butter
1 onion, finely chopped
s & p
2 cloves garlic, finely chopped
small handful fresh marjoram
2 cups sliced mushrooms
⅔ cup chicken livers
beef stock cube dissolved in a little water
6 pieces of filet steak
3 sheets puff pastry
1 egg, beaten for glaze

METHOD

Saute garlic, onion & mushrooms in oil & 2T of butter.
Season with s & p and cook until liquid is evaporated.
Finely chop chicken livers, add to th mushroom mixture
along with the marjoram and the beef stock. Simmer until
liquid is evaporated.
Sear steak quickly in rest of butter.
Divide mushroom mixture evenly amoung half a sheet of
pastry x 6. Place steak ontop, wrap up this in the pastry
pinching edges to seal. P lace on greased baking dish,
seam side down Glaze with beaten egg. Bake 15 mins
mod oven, or less if you want the steak to be pretty
pink in the middlxe. Rest 10 mins before serving.
You can use a beef tenderloin instead of fiet steak
and you can substitute the chicken livers for
prepared chicken liver pate.

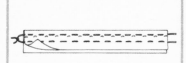

▲1. *Knot cords and trim lining tape at one end.*

▲2. *Pin and tack the tape*

▲3. *Neaten tape one side, free cords at the other*

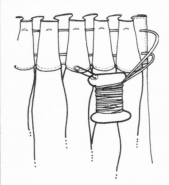

▲4. *Wind surplus cord on to a cord tidy*

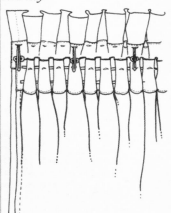

▲5. *Attach hooks to lining and curtain*

Make luxurious lined curtains and make them practical with detachable linings ▼ ▲

Tom's Spag Bol:

<u>Spaghetti Bolognaise</u>

3 cloves garlic, crushed
1 lg onion, finely diced
500 gms beef mince
3 lg flat field mushrooms
1T fresh oregano, finely chopped
1 tin Italian tomatoes
1 small can tomato paste
¼   salt & pepper
big splash red wine (cab sauv)

Saute garlic & onion in olive oil gently.
Add mince, brown.
Meanwhile in another frypan cook the sliced
mushrooms in butter until soft. Season with
salt & pepper.
Add mushrooms to mince mixture.
Add canned tomatoes, tomato paste, red wine
and oregano. Simmer about 45 mins on very low
heat. Serve over thin spaghetti noodles with
lots of grated parmesan cheese, & crusty bread.

Tom 'helping' me photograph a painting
Murdoch Rd, Grey Lynn, Auckland
NZ

Tom, & friend
East Cape, NZ.

Victorian (AUST)
Schoolboys Ruby
Union Emblem

Tom's bro - Dick, Melbourne

Roast lamb   (mum)

Place leg of Lamb in baking dish,
sprinkle liberally with salt & pepper
Spread 2 Tblsp flour over meat and in dish.
Add 2 oz butter.
Put in hot oven, 200°F for 15 mins.
Turn down to 150° and cook for a further 2 hours.
You may need a little longer depending on size of roast.
Add peeled potatoes, pumpkin, kumera and onion to roasting pan an hour
before meat is done, turning once whilst cooking.

Gravy:

Remove meat from dish and set aside to rest.
Place veg in oven dish and set aside in warming drawer.
Place roasting dish on stove top and turn element on to med.
Add 2tblsp flour and 2tblsp butter into dish.
Scrape bottom and sides to get all the flavourings while the butter is sizzling.
Cook the flour in the butter until it is a little browned, add cooking water from
any vegetables you are having or just boiling water from the jug.
Stir quickly with a fork mixing into an even paste, keep adding water until the
gravy is of a good consistency. Add plenty of salt & Pepper, add soya sauce or
vegemite, to colour and flavour. Worchestshire sauce could be used instead of
the soya sauce.
Pour into heated jug for serving.

Serve with peas, steamed broccoli , or creamed spinach.

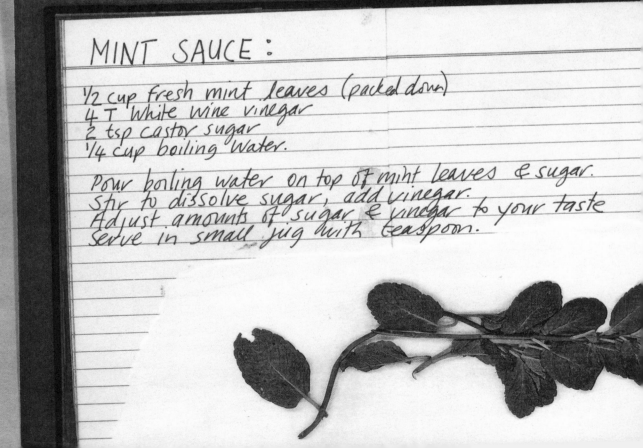

MINT SAUCE :

½ cup fresh mint leaves (packed down)
4 T white wine vinegar
2 tsp castor sugar
¼ cup boiling water.

Pour boiling water on top of mint leaves & sugar.
Stir to dissolve sugar, add vinegar.
Adjust amounts of sugar & vinegar to your taste
Serve in small jug with teaspoon.

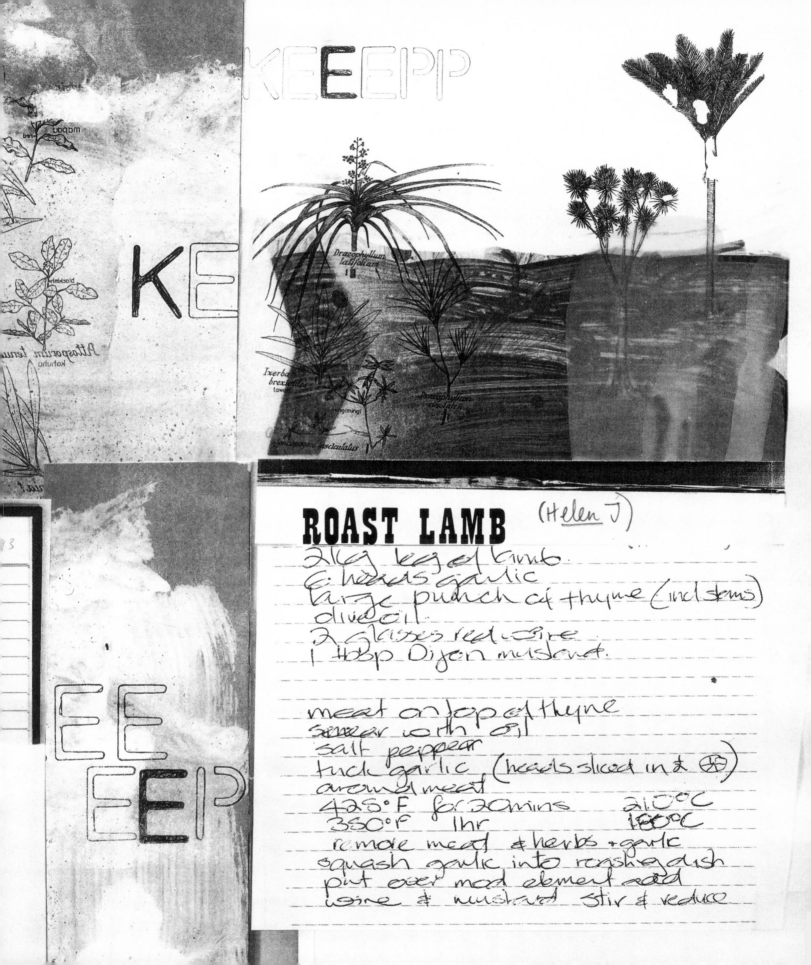

KEEEPP

KE

EE
EEP

ROAST LAMB (Helen J)

2kg leg of lamb
6 heads garlic
large punch of thyme (incl stems)
olive oil
2 glasses red wine
1 tbsp Dijon mustard.

meat on top of thyme
smear with oil
salt pepper
tuck garlic (heads sliced in ½ ⊕)
around meat
425°F for 20mins   210°C
350°F   1hr   180°C
remove meat & herbs + garlic
squash garlic into roasting dish
put over med element add
wine & mustard stir & reduce

aunts Hazel + centre ...

Bacon & Egg Pie   (aunty Hazel)
3Sheets of frozen puff pastry
250-350gms streaky bacon, thinly sliced
8 free range eggs (large)
1 lg tomato diced
½ onion, finely diced
S& pepper
beaten egg for wash
Grease oven dish with a little oil or
butter. ✗ Line bottom and sides with
2 sheets of the pastry.
Put dish on oven tray & cook 10 mins,
mod oven.
Take out &firmly push any risen pastry
back into place. Sprinkle bacon
over pastry, then break eggs directly
in, gently break yolks with a butter
knife so they spread a little. Sprinkle o
over tomatoes & onion. Season with plenty
of s&p. Put last sheet of pastry on top,
squash edges together with fork.
Brush with egg wash, make a few slashes
in top of pie for steam to escape.
Bake 30 mins @ 200. F or until top is
golden brown.
(this dish is excellent eaten cold on
picnics).

POST-SCRIPT   183

people show that there is greater genuine desire to understand
the mysteries of the deep than scholars and experts imagine.
In time, and as interest becomes more widespread, these
museums will multiply. And in their own no less effective way

Roast Pork, Crunchy Crackling and Apple Sauce

Buy either a boned and rolled Pork Loin or a small leg
(have butcher score the skin).

Rub skin with salt and oil. Melt some butter and oil in a meat
dish, place meat on top and sprinkle 1 tablespoon of flour in dish
around the meat. (This helps make nice gravy) Place in hot oven,
400°F and cook until crackling is crisp and crunchy, maybe 10 to 20
minutes depending on the oven.

Turn heat down to 300°F, (180°C) and cook meat long and slowly.
At least 2 to 3 hours depending on the size.
If crackling gets too dark cover lightly with foil.
The secret to a nice piece of pork is the long slow cooking
process. I like the meat so well cooked that it isn't dry,
but is hard to carve as it falls apart.

Apple sauce is a must and can be served
in a variety of ways. When in a hurry
tinned is good or if time allows stew some
Granny Smiths, add a little sugar and
a couple of cloves. Another alternative is
to place apple slices in with the meat for
the last 30 minutes of cooking.

Kumera, pumpkin, potatoes & small roasting onions
all cut up fairly small, can be added for the
last hour.
Remove the meat, turn the heat up and
finish the vegetables off until they are crisp.
I sometimes take the veggies out and put them
in another dish so that I can use the meat dish
to make the gravy.

Gravy: Strain most of the fat off leaving about
2 tblsp. Add 2 tlbsp of flour,
stir well including all the juices from the meat
and cook over low heat on top of stove for a
couple of minutes. Season well with S & P.
Strain any hot water from veggies into gravy,
otherwise use hot water. Using hot water stops
lumps forming. The taste comes from the meat and
veggies and the colour from the scrapings.
If gravy is not brown enough add a little vegemite.

mum, Fields
(NZ)

HI Fran,

It's Fran...here's Dad's Pork recipe,
it's a take on the traditional Italian Porchetta recipe,
but a lot easier, and just as yummy!

1 leg of free range pork, boned and rolled and tied
                       (your butcher should do this)
1 1/2 tsp Sea salt
1 Tbs Olive oil
3 cloves of Garlic
2 small onions
2 cups of red win
1 cup of water
A good hand full of fresh fennel fronds

Roast at 170 c allowing 30-35 minutes per 500g

Francesca's Father. (2nd from left) King Cross, Sydney 1962

Okay...using a sharp knife, score the rind, and preheat your oven to the highest setting. Then using a smaller knife, (paring knife) make at least 3 holes down into the meat on either end of the pork. They need to be big enough to get your index finger into. Now slice the garlic in half and stuff all six pieces into each hole, as far as your finger will go. Then divide the fennel into six smaller bunches and stuff them in after the garlic, it doesn't matter if the fennel is hanging out a bit, it just adds to the rustic nature of this dish! Now, rub the olive oil and salt onto the rind and all over the pork, if you have any small bits of fennel left, rub them on too.

Cut the onions in two even halves, no more than 2cm high, and place them on the baking tray to make a bed for the pork. Place the pork on top of the onions, and pour in the red wine and water, adjust the amount of wine and water according to the size of your meat, but there should be enough to at least cover the onions and touch the base of the pork.

Put in the oven and turn the heat down to 170 c, and cook until the internal temperature has reached 71-76 c. So if it's 1kg of pork, then around about an hour and a bit. Top up the liquid in the tray from time to time with a little water, you want it to reduce the liquid a lot, but not completely disappear! When cooked, take out of the oven, drain the liquid into a bowl and reserve for drizzling.

Now cover the pork with tin foil, and let the pork rest for at least 25mins. If your crackling is not crunchy enough, take the crackling off the meat and place it under the grill until puffy...YUM! There are always fights at my house over the crackling. Carve the meat into 2cm pieces, my Dad use to slice it quite thinly, but however you like it is fine. Then lay the meat on a warmed plate and take the reserved juices and drizzle over the meat. I like to serve this with mashed Kumera, (sweet potato).

Enjoy!Ciao, and buon appetito.
(see you at netball on Saturday)!
Fran x

TAGINE of LAMB

Tagine of lamb

1 tsp grd pepper
1½ tbsp paprika
1 tsp cumin ground
   " coriander "
1½ tbsp ground ginger
1 tbsp turmeric
2 tbsp ground cinnamon

Serves 4-6
Nice with Couscous

1 boned shoulder lamb cut into 5cm pieces
2 tbsp olive oil
1 large onion sliced finely
2 cloves of crushed garlic
500ml tomato juice
400g chopped tin tomatoes
120g dried apricots chopped
6 dates chopped
2 tbsp sultanas
½ cup almond flakes
1 tsp saffron threads
600ml chicken stock
2 tbsp chopped parsley

Combine spices and divide in two. Toss
lamb in one half cover + marinate
overnight in fridge

Heat 1 tbsp oil in casserole dish (which
can sit on element) cook onion til
softened. Add spice mix + cook, add
garlic.

Heat oil in new fry pan, brown lamb pieces.
Add lamb to tagine. Simmer 1 cup of
juice in frypan + pour over lamb
Add all remaining bring to lazy simmer
Cover with lid + bake at 150° for 2 or 2½
hours. Sprinkle with parsley.

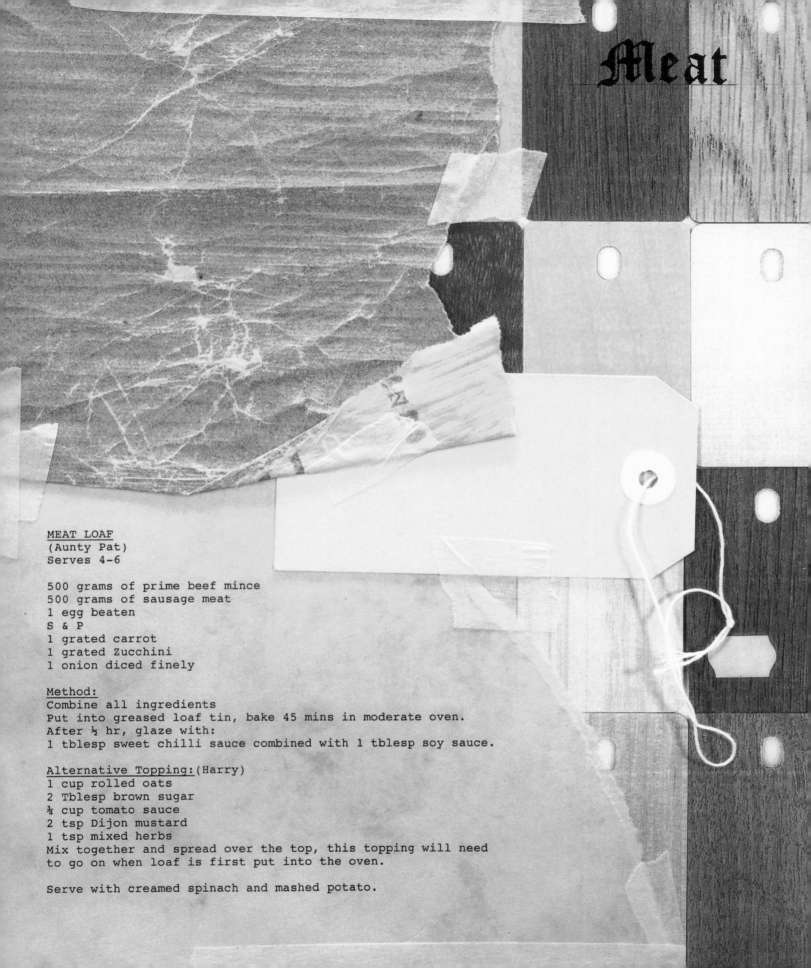

MEAT LOAF
(Aunty Pat)
Serves 4-6

500 grams of prime beef mince
500 grams of sausage meat
1 egg beaten
S & P
1 grated carrot
1 grated Zucchini
1 onion diced finely

Method:
Combine all ingredients
Put into greased loaf tin, bake 45 mins in moderate oven.
After ½ hr, glaze with:
1 tblesp sweet chilli sauce combined with 1 tblesp soy sauce.

Alternative Topping:(Harry)
1 cup rolled oats
2 Tblesp brown sugar
¼ cup tomato sauce
2 tsp Dijon mustard
1 tsp mixed herbs
Mix together and spread over the top, this topping will need
to go on when loaf is first put into the oven.

Serve with creamed spinach and mashed potato.

Aberdeen Sausage (Leiha)

1.lb Minced Steak, ½ lb Sausage meat, 1 cup breadcrumbs, 1 chopped onion, 1 Egg, any sauces, 1 Teaspoon Mixed herbs, Salt & pepper.
steam in basin 2hrs or bake in oven 1½hrs

Meat Loaf (Aunty Hazel)

½ lb Mince & Sausagemeat
1 cup Breadcrumbs.
1 Onion
1 Celery stalk
1 Apple
2 Tabs Chutney
1 Teaspoon W. Sauce
1 " Stock in 2 Tabs Boiling Water
Salt & Pepper
Tomato Sauce & Brown Sugar on Top

1 egg
Rasher Bacon
Grated Carrot
Cream.
Herbs

350 1hr.

Beef Stroganoff   (Mum)

500 grms of eye fillet steak
150 grms of mushrooms
2 tsp Worcestershire sauce
1 tblesp tomato paste
1 cup cream (lite is good)
or 1 small carton sour cream

Trim any fat from meat, cut into
thin strips and pepper and salt.
Heat a little oil and butter in
fry pan and brown meat quickly on
high heat. Remove and add finely
sliced mushrooms and cook until tender.
Return meat to pan, add Worcestershire
sauce & tomato paste, cook for 3 or
4 mins.
Add cream **or** carton of sour cream
and heat gently. Don't let it boil
or it will curdle.
Serve with mashed potatoes, pasta or rice.

For a change you can leave out
Worcestershire sauce and add lemon juice.
Finely sliced onions can be added with
mushrooms and chopped parsley sprinkled
on top is always nice. Alternatively
add ½ tsp finely chopped fresh thyme leaves,
cooked in with the meat.

Floodstack
Lucky

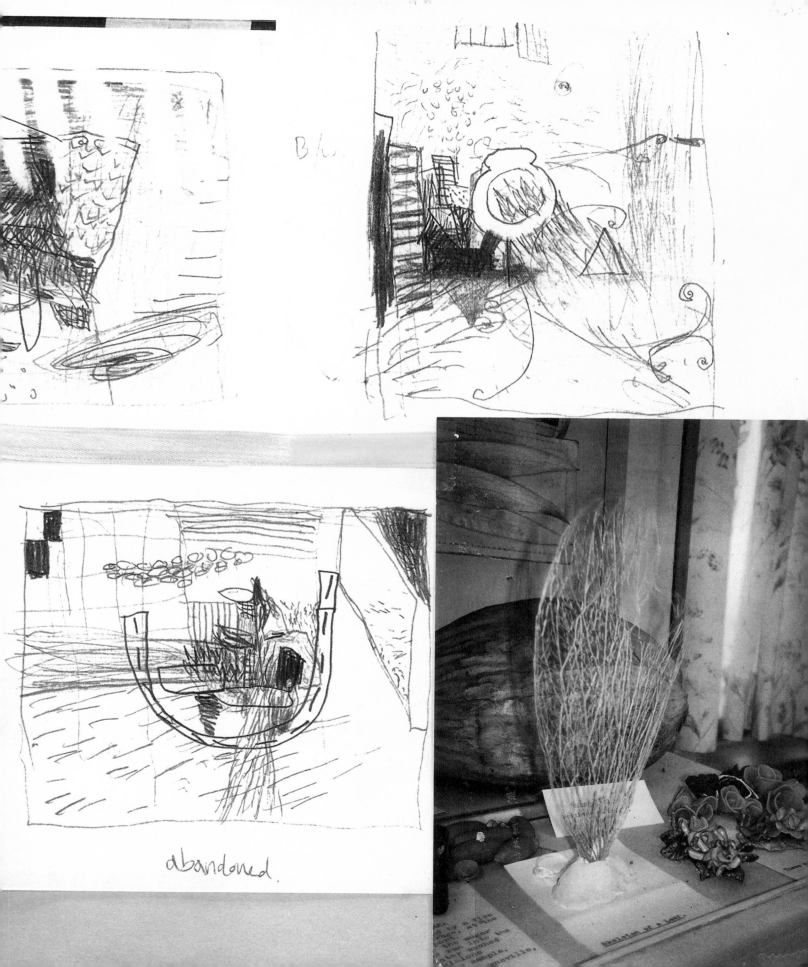

B/W.

abandoned

Handy Hints:

- Burnt onions = bitterness. Slow & gentle saute = sweet.

- Mashed carrots & parsnips are surprising delicious.

- Lemon, ginger & honey. makes a very soothing hot drink for a sore throat.

- Lemon juice squeezed over parsley over vegetables helps absorb vitamen C.

- Roasted garlic becomes quite nutty.

- Peel onions with the tap running → stops the tears.

- Poached eggs will stay together if vinegar is added.

BEEF CURRy (Louise)

Brown 1 Kg Skirt Steak and 3 Onions in Ghee, garlic and 2 heaped tsp of ginger.

Add 1/2 jar Madras curry paste
3 tablespoons tomato   paste
2 tablespoons hot Mango chutney
1 tsp cumin
1 tsp coriander
1 tsp tumeric
1 tsp cardamom
1 tsp cayenne pepper
1 tsp garam masala
2 Bay leaves

Add 1 can coconut milk
500g frozen beans
a squeeze of lemon juice

Bake for 2 hours @180

Shepherd's Pie

Ingredients:
1 kg beef mince
2 cloves garlic crushed
2 smallish onions diced
2 carrots peeled and sliced finely on an angle
1½ cups mushrooms sliced
1 cup peas
1 can Italian tomatoes crushed
2 T tomato paste
2 T soy sauce
dash worchestshire sauce
salt & pepper
2 cups veg or beef stock
water
small handful of fresh parsley & thyme chopped finkely
For the potato topping:
4-5 medium potatoes. peeled & boiled til soft
2T butter
½ cup milk
s &p
METHOD:
Cook onion, garlic in 2 T olive oil. add mince, brown.
add all the rest of the ingredients, simmer slowly for an hour.
You may need to adjust seasonings. Also if you like a thicker
consistency to the mince, strain off some of the liquid and mix
in 1-2 T of plain flour, slowly stir this back into the mince.
Should thicken nicely.
Topping:
Mash potatoes with butter, milk, s&p.
At this stage you can addin:
Heaps of chopped parsley and more finely diced onion
or
2 T good horseradish & cream instead of the milk
or
1 T seeded or dijohn mustard and replace the milk with sourcream
Pile potato mix ontop of the savoury mince, that you have already
placed into a deepish baking dish.
Into the oven. moderate temp. 40 mins.
MINCE PIE
Replace the mashed potato with sheets of puff pastry - brush with
egg before putting into hot oven. Pie is done when pastry is golden.
Sadie & Bede love to have their own individual pies baked in small
ramekins.

Mum (Trip to Sydney 1966 or 67.) →

THREE SISTERS, KATOOMBA, N.S.W.

TE AROHA 1969

Leila   Tracey   Francis   Joanne

HOKEY POKEY BISCUITS

8 oz butter
1 c. sugar
2-½ c. flour (wholemeal)
2 tsp Baking Powder
Pinch salt
2 Tble sps Milk
  "   GOLDEN SYRUP.
1 heaped tsp. Baking
                    Soda
NB Honey can be used instead of GOLDEN S.

Cream Butter & Sugar
Warm Milk & Golden
Sydney in pot, add
baking soda and
mix well until frothy.
Add to butter & sugar
mix. Stir in flour,
baking powder & salt.
Roll into small
balls, press down
with fork and
cook at 350° 10-20 min

love the typo

AFGHANS (Mege)

200g (7ozs)	Butter	25 (1oz) Cocoa
75g (3ozs)	Sugar	50g (2oz) Cornflake
175g (6ozs)	Flour	

Soften butter add sugar & beat to cream
add flour, cocoa & cornies.
Bake 15' @ 180°C (350°F)

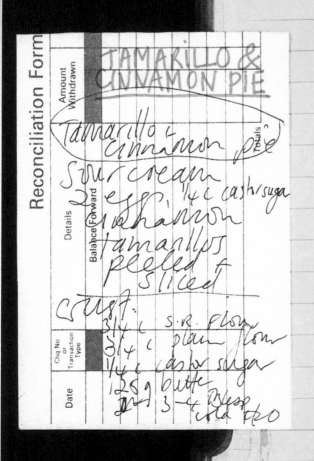

Reconciliation Form

TAMARILLO & CINNAMON PIE

Tamarillo & cinnamon pie

Sour cream
2 eggs, 1/4 c castr sugar
cinnamon
tamarillos peeled & sliced

Crust:
3/4 c S.R. flour
3/4 c plain flour
1/4 c castr sugar
125g butter
3-4 tblsp cold H2O

Feijoa loaf

1 c feijoa chopped
1 c boiling H2O
1 c sugar
2 oz butter

Boil for 5 mins stirring

Cool + beat in 1 egg, add vanilla essence

1 tsp BP, **2 C Flour**
1 tsp B. soda

350° for 45 mins

Rocky Road
Cut up 2 pkts
Marshmellows,
Brazil nuts, Cherries
Melt ige cake
dark chocolate
with 1 oz cofa,
add 1 tols of
sherry Pour over
& keep in fridge

NINETTE DE VALOIS

in Coppéli

TATIANA RIABOUCHINSKA

in The Blue Bird

BUTTER SCOTCH SLICE

Butterscotch Slice

4 oz butter (or marg) 1 cup S.R. Flour.

2 oz sugar

(I often use some grated lemon peel
and/or a teaspoon vanilla for flavouring)
Cream butter + sugar - add flour. Press
into slice tin. — Moderate oven 15-20 mins

Filling or Topping.

4 rounded tablespoons icing sugar
3 teaspoons golden syrup
2 tablespoons butter (or marg)
Put topping into a saucepan as slice is put
into oven. Stir over gentle heat until butter
melts and all is well mixed. DO NOT BOIL.
Pour over biscuit base while it is hot.
Cut into slices while still warm, but leave
in tin until cold.

Store in airtight tin. Will keep for
weeks (if the family lets it.)

I found this recipe
in Mum's Scrapbook,
I don't recognize the
handwriting....

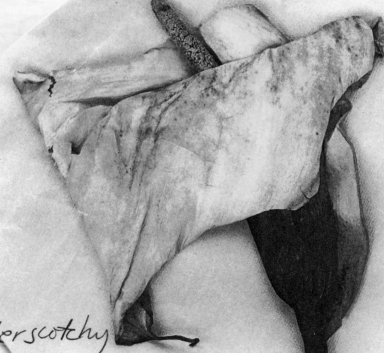

... but I recognize
the slice! The
combination of golden
syrup + icing sugar
works really well.
- moreish, chewy + butterscotchy

FIG. 9

Blanket stitch in thick wool is worked all round the pram cover shown above. The decoration
is in daisy stitch. When plain blanket stitch has been learned, it is interesting to work alternate
long and short stitches, but many different arrangements may be made.

Queen Cakes (madeira cake) (Lee)

2oz butter, ½ cup sugar, 2 eggs, 1½ cups flour
2 teaspoons baking powder, ¼ teaspoon salt,
½ teaspoon lemon essence, 2 tablespoons milk.
Combine these ingredients by the Buttercake
Method. place in pattypan hollows and
bake at 400° farenheight for 20 minutes till
lightly browned and cooked. (ice with Buttericing)
N.B By putting in 8" baking tin you have a
madeira cake – Bake at (375) 375 for 30–40 minutes
(Do not ice.)

currant cakes

follow Queen Cakes recipe, add 1 teaspoon
of golden syrup and ½ cup currants with the
lemon essence.

Cakes

pudding

biscu

doughs
pikelets
pancake
scone

Pikelets.
(Aunty Hazel)

1 Egg	Tablespoon Butter.
Pinch Salt.	Tablespoon Sugar
1½ Cups Flour	2 Teaspoons Baking Powder.
½ Cup Milk.	

Beat egg & sugar, stir in Flour & Milk.
Melt Butter & pour in, then B.P. Last.

Queen Cakes.

2. Eggs.	1. Tablespoon Butter.
½ Cup Sugar	1. Heaped Cup Flour.
1. Teaspoon B.P.	Currants.
Lemon Essence.	

Cream butter & sugar, add beaten eggs, then
Flour in which B.P. is mixed, lastly essence
& currants. Bake in good oven.

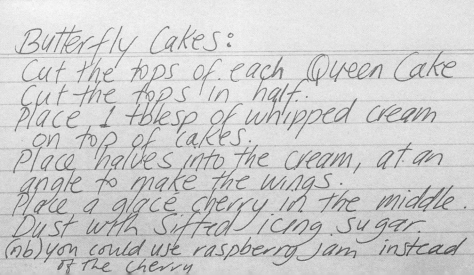

Butterfly Cakes:
Cut the tops of each Queen Cake
Cut the tops in half.
Place 1 tblesp of whipped cream
on top of cakes.
Place halves into the cream, at an
angle to make the wings.
Place a glacé cherry in the middle.
Dust with sifted icing sugar.
(nb) you could use raspberry jam instead
of the cherry

LEMON MERINGUE PIE

Pastry:
4oz flour
2oz butter
2 T iced water
pinch salt
Sift flour & salt, rub in butter, mix to a smooth
dough with a little water.
Line a flan tin and bake 10 – 15 mins at 370F

Filling:
Heat 14 oz milk and 1 oz butter in saucepan.
Beat 2 egg yolks & 2 heaped T castor sugar
until thick.
Fold in 2 T plain flour, stir in 1 cup milk gradually
over low heat stirring for 2-3 mins, add in zest and
juice of 1 lemon, pour into pastry base.

Meringue:
Whip 2 egg whites until they form stiff peaks, slowly add
4 T castor sugar. Pile on top of custard filling and cook
7 -10 minutes, moderate oven.

Dorset Apple cake   (Mum)
                    → Jo → me
1 cup flour
1½ tsp BP
Salt
¼ tsp cinnamon
¼ cup sugar
50 g butter
1 apple
¼ cup currants
1 Dsp Brown sugar
¼ cup milk
- sift dry ingredients into a
bowl. Cut in butter, peel, core
+ chop apple. stir in white
sugar, apple + currants to dry
ingredients. blend in milk to
make a drop batter. Spread
mixture in bottom of buttered
dish. Sprinkle with brown
sugar. Bake 20 mins
                    Oven 400°F
                    200°C

(This cake is good served hot
(with ice cream.)

beat together and boil like

lorraine Carol Bull
lorraine Carol Bull.

mum (19 years)

LARGE CHOCOLATE CKE

4 eggs (room temp)

2 cups ᵪ̶ᵪ̶ᵪ̶ᵪ̶ sugar
8 oz butter
~~4 T butter~~
4 T golden syrup
4 T cocoa
4 tsp baking powder ⎤ sifted
2 cups flour   ⎦
2 tsp vanilla
4 tsp baking soda
3 cups milk (golden)
Melt butter & golden syrup.
beat eggs & sugar well → add butter + G.S.
Sift cocoa, baking powder
& flour together, add to mixture
along with vanilla,
Soak soda in milk, leave till
last, add to mixture, mix well
Line a 23cm high sided square tin
with baking paper.
Pour cake mixture into tin & bake
1hr & 20 mins @ 165 degrees.
When cooked, remove cake from tin
leave to cool upside down.
ICING:
4 oz butter
2 cups icing sugar
1 T. cocoa
2 T. boiling water
1 tsp vanilla
Melt butter, beat ingredients
together.
This cake freezes well

special note:
This cake is solid &
moist- making it easy
to carve into and
create fancy, fun
birthday cakes, I
have made... a castle
a jet fighter, an octopus
a dump truck & a train.

Fashion Jewelry

$2.00

MADE IN CHINA

For Franni

2Choc. Biscuit Fudge
Ingredients:
175 g butter
½ cup sugar
4T cocoa
1 egg, beaten   1T FLOUR (heaped)
250g pkt round wine or vanilla
wine biscuits, crushed.
Method:
Melt tog. butter, sugar & cocoa,
stirring constantly for 3-5 mins.
Mix in egg & biscuits. & Flour
Press into greased tin,
bake 20 mins, mod oven.
Ice with chocolate icing
Sprinkle with cocnut.
          Coconut

en Anniversaire   ma Cherie

CARROT & APPLE CAKE (lg)

¾ C Raw Sugar
8 oz Butter
3 eggs
2½ C wholemeal flour (S.R.)
2 tsp. B.P., pinch salt

2 Tblesp. Milk
2 tsp baking soda
3 medium carrots (grated)
1 lg apple, sliced thinly
          & stewed
½ c. chopped walnuts
½ c. honey
     Cream tog. butter &
sugar, beat in honey,
stir in sifted flour, B.P.
& salt. Add beaten
eggs. Warm milk &
add baking soda stir
frothy mixture into
butter & sugar mixture.
Add carrot, apple &
walnuts, bake in greased
tin and at 375° for 1hr.
check after 3/4 hr.
Ice with lemon
          icing

GINGER SLICE (Jo.)

SPICE

INGREDIENTS:
1 cup sugar
1/2 cup milk
1/4 tin condensed milk
1 Tblesp. Golden Syrup
4 ozs butter
METHOD:
Boil above ingredients
together slowly, for
15 minutes.
Add 1 packet crushed
gingernuts & 1 tsp
vanilla.
Press into greased slice
tin — Refridgerate.
TOP: with toasted,
chopped nuts.

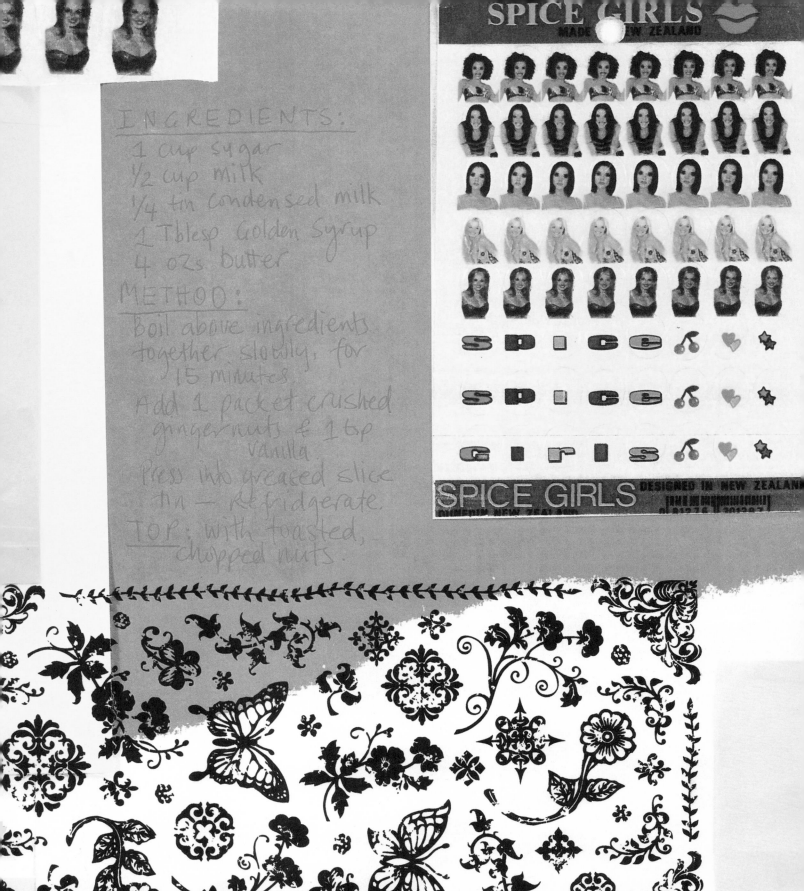

SPICE GIRLS
MADE ... NEW ZEALAND

SPICE
SPICE
GIRLS

SPICE GIRLS   DESIGNED IN NEW ZEALAND
DUNEDIN NEW ZEALAND

NEW ZEALAND

NEW ZEALAND

TUTAKI, PENRHYN ISLANDS, NIUE, RARATONGA

$4

Tracey,s Boiled Fruit Loaf

This is a super-qiuck, fail proof recipe, which works no matter
whatxdried fruit you have in the cupboard. I like it because it is reasonably
healthy.

one cup chopped fruit:
dates, apricots, sultanas, dried apple, pear, currents etc.
one cup boiling water
one cup raw sugar
one tblesp golden syrup
one oz butter
one teasp baking soda
2 cups wholemeal flour
Place all ingredientsin bowl except flour. Pour water over. Cool
Add flour
Bake in greased loaf tin, 350 degrees for one hr.

Raisin Loaf

2 c Flour
dash salt
3 tsp baking powder
3/4 c sugar
1 c raisins   1 c milk
2 Tblesp golden syrup
- Sift dry ingredients into
bowl, add sugar + raisins
Heat milk and g.syrup, pour
into flour mix. stir, bake 350°- 1 hr

BRIDGE OVER TROUBLE WATER

G   G   C   G   C

When you're weary, feelin' small,

F   C   G   C   G   C   G   C   G

When tears are in your eyes, I'll dry them all;

D   Em   D

I'm on your side.

D7   G   G7   G9   C   A   D

Oh, when times get rough, and friends just can't be found,

G7   G9   C   A   G   E9   E7   C   B7   Em

Like a bridge over trouble water,   I will lay me down.

G   C   G   E7   C   D7   G

Like a bridge over trouble water, I will lay me down.

When you're down and out, when you're on the street,
When evening falls so hard I'll comfort you.
I'll take your part.
Oh, when darkness comes and pain is all around,
Like a bridge over trouble water I will lay me down,
Like a bridge over trouble water I will lay me down.

Sail on silver girl, sail on by.
Your time has come to shine.
All your dreams are on their way.
See how they shine.
Oh, if you need a friend I'm sailing right behind.
Like a bridge over trouble water I will ease your mind,
Like a bridge over trouble water I will ease your mind.

Lorraine Carol Bull / HANSEN.
EKETAHUNA. 1959

IDEAS FOR AFTERNOON TEAS

THAMES VALLEY STUDIOS

PHONE 820   P.O. BOX 102

TE AROHA

SAVOURY SNACKS

Beat an egg, make it thick with grated cheese.
Spread over 4 slices of bread, grill until
puffy & golden.

SAVOURY ROLLS

Use thinly sliced white bread, crusts cut off.
Spread with any of the following mixes:
-grated cheese & onion
-savory mince
-smoked salmon, cream cheese & capers
-grated cheese and tinned crushed pineapple
                        (drained)
Spread 1T of filling along along top third
of slice of bread, roll up & press edges
 to hold. Straight into hot oven, 220 F.
until golden brown.

SAVOURY EGGS

6 hard boiled eggs, shelled & halved.
scrape out yolks, mash with the following:
1T softened butter.   1T mayonnaise
salt & pepper   ½-1 tsp mustard
Pile mix back into empty halved egg whites.
Alternative addings: finely chopped parsley
½ tsp good curry powder instead of the mustard.

SCONES & EGG

Batch of freshly made scones
halved & buttered.
Use same egg mix as for savory eggs,
adding in the egg whites as well.
Pile mix on top of scones, be generous.
Sprinkle with snipped chives or parsley.
Eaten cold.

APPLE SHORTCAKE
(Aunty Leila)

200gms butter } cream & add in
1/2 cup sugar } 1 beaten egg
Add 1½ cups flour & 1 tsp baking powder.
Divide mixture in half. spread out first half
in bottom of greased pie dish — bake 10 mins.
Filling: Peel core & slice 4-5 apples, simmer
in 1 cup of water, 1T sugar & 2 cloves.
Drain well, remove cloves.
Spread filling over partially cooked base.
Spread rest of pastry mixture on top, sprinkle
with sugar — cook 40 mins, mod'oven.
Perfect for picnics.

My younger
sister - Jo
& I at a
picnic at
Karangahake
Gorge (1972)
The apple
shortcake
was made
by my Aunty
Edith & is
under the
ballerina
tray. →

Pavlova   (Mum)
4 Eggs, separated
Make sure there is NO yolk in with
the whites when you separate them.
Also, eggs must be at room temperature,
(at least 2 hrs out of fridge).
Beat egg whites until stiff.
Slowly add:
1 cup of castor sugar
1 Tblsp water
1 tsp vanilla
1 tsp vinegar
With a spatula, quickly pile mixture onto
greased oven tray. Place in hot oven and
turn down to 150 degrees for 1 hour.
Turn oven off and leave there to cool.

Notes:
If you like a marshmellowy centre -pile high,
if you want the pavlova more crunchy, spread
the mixture out, flatten it more, before baking.
Decorate with whipped cream and your choice of:
passionfruit pulp, slices of peeled kiwifruit,
chocolate sprinkles, fresh berries or mango.

MARGOT FONTEYN

in Nocturne

Lemon Delicious (Helen)
Ingredients:
1 Tblsp butter   ¾ cup sugar
2 Tblsp flour   2 eggs
1 cup milk   1 lemon
Method:
Cream butter & sugar, add flour,
grated lemon rind and juice,
egg yolks and lastly milk.
When mixed add stiffly beaten egg whites.
Pour into greased dish
and bake in tray of water.
325°F, for one hour.

MARY HONER

in The Swan Lake

BREAD & BUTTER PUDDING

Cinnamon Mist T115-1

Bleached Canvas T115-2

INGREDIENTS:

8 slices of stale bread
4 eggs - beaten
60g butter
3 Tblesp brown sugar
1 cup milk
¼ cup raisins
2-3 drops vanilla essence

METHOD:

- Butter the slices of bread, sprinkle with brown sugar and cut each slice in ½
- Push firmly into a greased deep-oven dish.
- mix eggs, milk & vanilla together
- Pour over bread
- Bake 45 mins in mod. oven (sprinkle raisins throughout)

Stand Pudding in water bath while baking

Lorraine this is a lovely sweet and can be made day before or if in rush an hour before.

ALTERNATIVES:
- use golden syrup instead of Brown Sugar
- spread the bread with raspberry jam instead of Brown sugar + add handful of raisins, currants or sultanas
- sprinkle top with coconut or almonds.

BANANA SPLITS WITH HOT CHOCOLATE SAUCE

SAUCE: 1/2 Cup golden Syrup
       2 Tblesp. butter
       1/4 cup condensed milk
melt these 3 ingredients together in a small pot
Add: 1/4 cup cocoa dissolved in 2 tblesp. hot water
add 1/2 cup milk- stir until bubbling, pour hot over ice cream
SPLITS: 1 Banana per person, vanilla ice cream, HOT CHOC SAUCE
       Toasted nuts; peanuts or slivered almonds or coco
       nut
       Pink ice cream wafers, cut into triangles, cherries.
METHOD: Split bananas lengthways, place 2 scoops ice cream
       inbetween the banana slices, pour on HOT sauce. Sprinkle with
       nuts, add wafers, top with cherry.

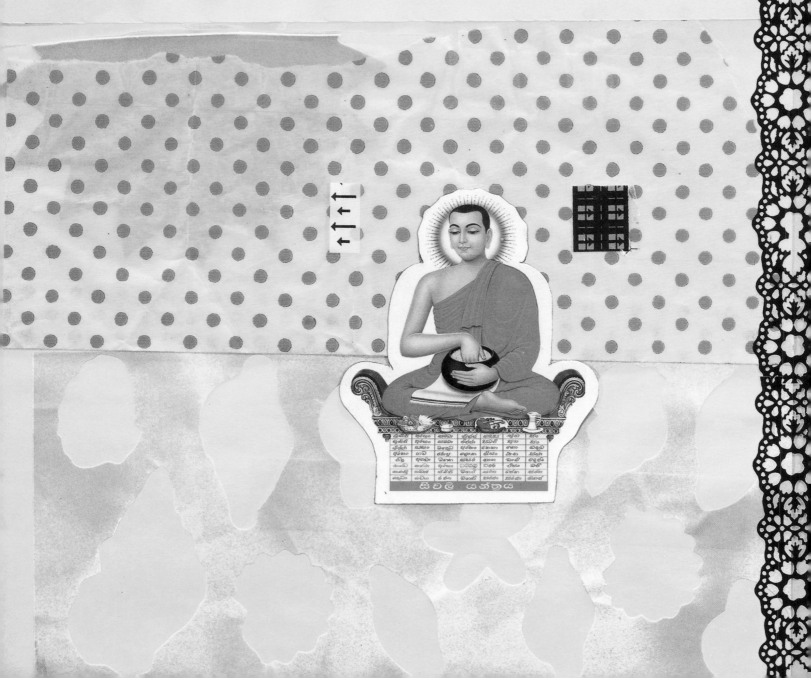

cont.... (& Feijoas)
Stew apples with
Sugar & Lemon juice
Slice bananas, mix in with
apples.

Add rest of dry ingrediants
to flour & butter mixture.
Put FRIUT in bottom of dish
Crumble the crumble

on top, press down firmly
Bake 30 mins, mod oven
untilX Golden browm on top.
        Brown

Feijoa and Banana Crumble (Serves 6)

150g flour
115g butter, softened and cut into small pieces
3 Tbs soft brown sugar
3 Tbs ground almonds
2 large cooking apples
1 Tbs castor sugar
1½ Tbs lemon juice
2 ripe but firm bananas
2 feijoas

Sift the flour into a bowl. Drop the butter
cubes into the flour and use two knives to cut it
through the flour until the pieces of butter are like
cornflakes------

cont..

Pip pip: perfect passionfruit

☐ Mix yoghurt and passionfruit pulp

SUNDRIES

at Uncle Kevins + Aunty Ediths 1968/9?
farm Morrinsville

ALMONDS	GROUND ALMONDS	ARROWROOT	DRIED APRICOTS	BAKING POWDER	BARLEY
DRIED BEANS	BICARBONATE OF SODA	BISCUITS	SAVOURY BISCUITS	BOUQUET GARNI	BRAN
BREADCRUMBS	CARAWAY SEEDS	CEREAL	CHERRIES	CHOCOLATE	DRINKING CHOCOLATE
COCOA	COCONUT	COFFEE	COFFEE BEANS		CORNFLAKES
CORNFLOUR	CREAM CRACKERS	CREAM OF TARTAR	CRISPBREADS	CRISPS	CURRANTS
CUSTARD POWDER	DATES	PLAIN FLOUR	SELF-RAISING FLOUR	STRONG FLOUR	WHOLEMEAL FLOUR
DRIED FRUITS	GELATINE	GRAVY POWDER	HORLICKS	LENTILS	MACARONI
MATZO MEAL	MILK POWDER	MIXED PEEL	MUESLI	NOODLES	NUTS
MIXED NUTS	OATS	DRIED ONIONS	OVALTINE	PARMESAN	PEANUTS
POPPY SEEDS	INSTANT POTATO	PRUNES	RAISINS	RICE CRISPIES	PATNA RICE
PUDDING RICE	SALT	SEA SALT	SEMOLINA	SESAME SEEDS	SOUP MIX
SPAGHETTI	SPLIT PEAS	STOCK CUBES	SUET	SUGAR	BROWN SUGAR
CASTOR SUGAR	DEMERARA SUGAR	ICING SUGAR	SULTANAS	TAPIOCA	
	DRIED VEGETABLES	WALNUTS	WEETABIX	WHEATGERM	DRIED YEAST
ALLSPICE	BASIL	BAY LEAVES	CARDAMOM	CAYENNE PEPPER	CELERY
CHILI POWDER	CHIVES	CINNAMON	CORIANDER	CLOVES	CUMIN
CURRY POWDER	DILL	FENNEL	GARLIC SALT	GINGER	MACE
MARJORAM	MINT	MIXED HERBS	MIXED SPICE	MUSTARD	NUTMEG
ONION SALT	OREGANO	PAPRIKA	PARSLEY	PEPPER	PEPPERCORN
PICKLING SPICE	ROSEMARY	SAFFRON	SAGE	TARRAGON	THYME

chocolate

*** really yummy
mmm

Chocolate fudge pudding:

cream 2 tbs ~~softened~~ butter
& 3/4 cup sugar, add one egg
vanilla, 1/2 cup milk, add 1
cup flour, 1 tsp B.P., 1 tbs
cocoa

place in greased pie dish
& mix in another basin
3/4 cup brown sugar, 3 tsp
cocoa, vanilla, 2 cups boiling
water, mix well pour over pie
dish mixture.
Bake. 50 mins in mod oven
(yummy)
350°

? — T.V. Toffee:
8Tbs sugar) Boil 5-6 mins
2Tbs vinegar) test in water
2Tbs Butter)
put to set in patty pans

Baked Custard

Baked Custard.
3 eggs, ¼ cup sugar,
Vanilla, 2 cups milk.
Beat tog, put in pyrex
dish, cover with tinfoil,
put in frypan of
hot water & cook 1 hrs
at 260°

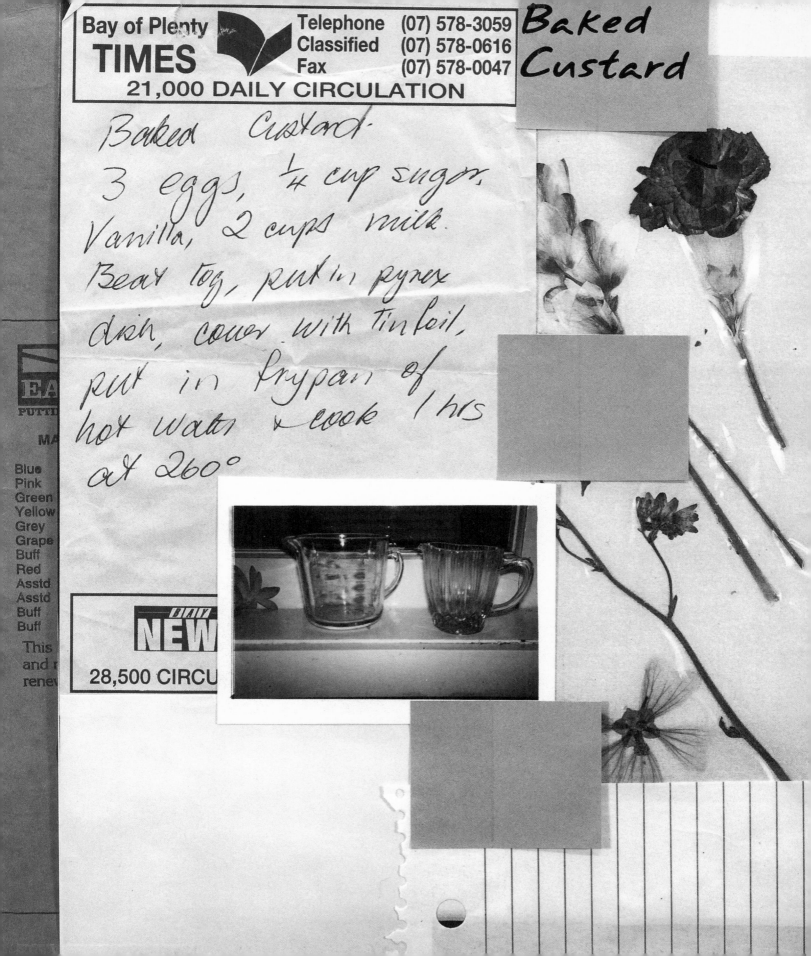

Aunty Hazel
was my godmother,
she cooked a fair
few things
excellently.

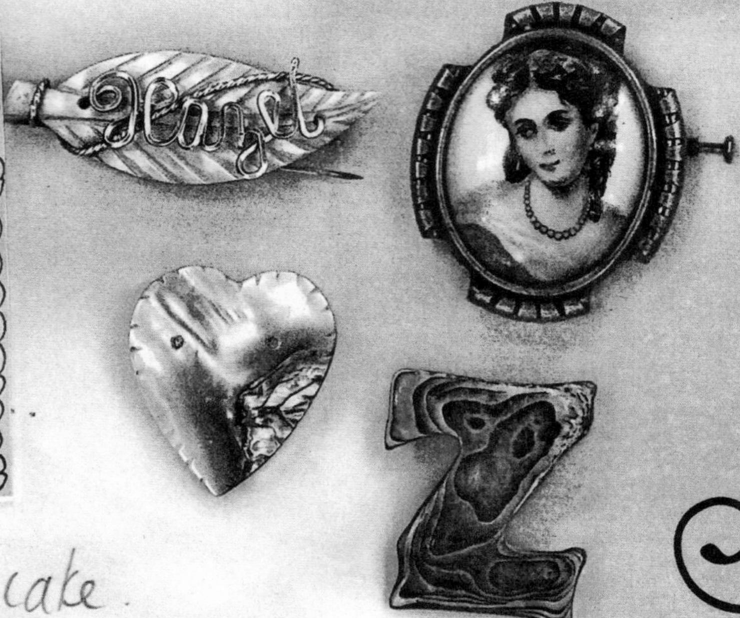

Aunty Hazel's cheesecake.

3 oz butter
1 packet 'Nice' Biscuits
½ tsp ground ginger
* Melt butter - add to crushed biscuits + ginger
Cook in oven at 350°c for 10 mins.
    Refrigerate

Filling: 250 gms cream cheese
    14 oz tin of condensed milk
    1 TBlesp. lemon rind
    ½ cup lemon juice
    10 oz carton sour cream
Mix cream cheese, gradually
add sour cream, condensed milk
rind & juice of lemon
    Dust with lemon
    - Refrigerate until set.

handy hint:
To cut a clean
slice - dip your
large sharp knife
into hot water
first.

Hazel

Bike
Decorating
Day

(Hazel ↑)

Jas. S. Lockley Ltd
P.O. Box 3445
Auckland

Hazel
at
Mission
Bay

Rice Pudding

Ingredients:

- 2 Tblesp. short grain rice (rinsed)
- 600ml milk
- 25g sugar
- ½ tsp vanilla essence

Method:

Place all ingredients into shallowish
pie dish, mix gently with fork.

Bake: 2 hrs @ 150°C or 275°F

Check after 1½ hrs incase you have
a hotter oven. - For a faster method. use
2 cups cooked rice & 2 eggs (beaten)
add the rice & eggs to the milk & sugar
Bake 45 mins   mod. oven.

Optional Extras: * grate fresh nutmeg over the top
* Drizzle Golden Syrup over the top
   half-way through baking
* Sprinkle with coconut & chopped nuts-
   macadamias or brazils, or slivered almonds

Sponge For Hot Fruit

Ingredients:
2 eggs
1/2 cup castor sugar
2/3 cup flour
1 tsp baking powder
Method:
Beat eggs and sugar together
until thickened add dry ingredients,
Pour over hot fruit
Bake half hour at 350F
Hot Fruit Suggestions:
Stewed apple with cloves,
plums, nectarines, tamarillos,
rhubarb, apple & boysenberries,
peaches, guavas, pears.

YOU'RE A FLAME IN MY HEART

What does that bunch signify? Here's a
fun guide to the flowers you've been
given:

Asters: symbols of love, and daintiness
Camellia (*pink*): longing for a man
Camellia (*red*): you're a flame in my heart
Gladiolus: love at first sight
Hydrangea: frigidity
Calla Lily: beauty
Carnation, (*pink*): I'll never forget you
Carnation, (*red*): my heart aches for you
Carnation, (*white*): sweet and lovely
White Lily: virginity, purity
Rose, (*red*): deep love
Rose, (*yellow*): decreasing love, jealousy
Rose, (*pink*): perfect happiness
Rose, (*white*): innocence and purity
Sunflowers: vitality
Violet, (*blue*): watchfulness, faithfulness

Mums multi
Fish Oil Tabs.
Coffee
Porridge
Apricots & Linseed
Wholemeal flour
Spinich.
W.W x4
W.B.
Rice.

coffee + milk
icecreams
lemoninade
natural yog.
eggs.

throaties
spiralina
sp.

Sausage
cheese
~~Mayo~~
yogurt.
Coffee
herbal T
corn chips
?
Fruit + ve

LKK THAI
Pork
LKK SING

STREAKY BACON
EGGS.
PUFF PASTRY.
CREAM.
BAKING SODA.
GROUND GINGER
RAISINS.
SWEET BREAD

ONION.
EGG WHITE.
BUTTER.
FLOUR
W.W.T.
ICE BREAD.

garlic
onions
aubergine
mushroom
toms
avacado

buttermilk
pasta
bacon
dried apricot

Steak
chicken wing
cream
eggs
potato
onion
hand soap - liquid
shampoo
pasta

cappucino
coffee

Dine
GARLIC
Barbacue
chicken
Feta cheese

Tacos.
Cooked chic
life jackets
linen

2 tin chikpeas.
Soup pasta.

Caster Sugar
butter 450g
Milk chocolate 250g
Chocolate chips
Milk
Sour
mixed spice

- dishwashing liqu
- cereal for Fee
- Juices
- Lemon & barle
- Fabric Softener (Next

olives
- Cucumber
- Lemons
- Pineapple
- Strawberries
- Chips
- Dips
- Cream cheese
- 2x Crunchies
- milk
- Bread

3 fish
1 sasage
2 fritters

3 fish
2 sasages
3 fritters
chips

Buns
Cheese
Eggs
Milk
red wine
Tomatoes
snail pell

IRN
magn

dishwash
bread
milk
basil
Brie
Mandar
sour crea
munc

Biscuits
Vaseline
NUTS RAISIN
medicine
Putty
NANAS
PEANUT BUTTER
Spuds

Cheese
Salad
few
wraps
Salads
Bread

bircher meusli
Hettberes

Chicken
Mesculun
cucumber
tomatoes
Brie x2
Cajun seasoning rub?
avocado
Ciabatta
dressing   avocado
           - mayo garlic

beer

burritos
basil
cheese
eggs
Bacon
Hash browns (wattis)
puffups
Loo paper
marmalade
Peanut butter
Butter
Margerine
milk
bread

Cans:
Tuna
Beetroot
peas
Loo paper
mushrooms
noodles
Beetroot

Meat
Casserole
steak
1kg
for lunch
monday

eggs
cr. ch
sour cr
serloin
humus
Chicken nee
capers
olives
pine nuts
walnu
lettuce

Prunes
Yogurt
Kumara
Bread

Acknowledgements

Thanks firstly, to my sister Fleur for suggesting the idea of developing my recipe book / wedding gift to her into a published book and to Pippa Masson from Curtis Brown for taking up the idea with such enthusiasm. Thanks to Paul McNally from Hardie Grant Books, it has been a pleasure to work with you, in my experience it is rare to work collaboratively with such ease. Thanks for your support and useful advice. Thank you Mr John Collie for being such an excellent photographer, so thorough and particular, you make my images look amazing! Thanks to my Mum, for teaching me to cook and for sharing her recipes and photographs, and to my Aunty Hazel and Aunty Pat, (both now passed) whose recipe books I have consulted continuously. Thanks also to my sisters, other family members and friends who have shared their recipes and /or their artworks. Special thanks to Tom, my partner, and Sadie & Bede, my children, who have given me the space, time and encouragement to complete this project.

Published in 2011 by Hardie Grant Books

Hardie Grant Books 85 High Street Prahran, Victoria 3181
www.hardiegrant.com.au

Cataloguing-in-Publication data is available from the National Library of Australia.

ISBN: 978 1742701158

Published by Paul McNally
Design, collage and layout by Frances Hansen
Cover design by Heather Menzies
Layout photography by John Collie
Colour reproduction by Splitting Image Colour Studio
Printed in China by 1010 Printing International Limited